# In Praise

"Laura Stinchfield is ‹             ……. ᴿead this book and she
will be a treasure in plain sight. Chock full of remarkable, enlightening and sometimes startling anecdotes, *Voices of the Animals*
can steer us all to deeper connections with our pets, with other
people and with ourselves. Laura's insights into animal behavior
can be, if taken to heart, nothing short of revolutionary. Let this
book change your life. Keep it close and read and re-read and
re-read. Wake up!"

— **Caroline Thompson,** screenwriter of *Edward Scissorhands,*
*Homeward Bound: The Incredible Journey* and
screenwriter/director of *Black Beauty*

"Laura has been blessed with an amazing and very special gift!
I've known and worked with her for many years in both a professional and personal capacity. Her lovely book will make you laugh
out loud and pull at your heart strings at the same time. Laura's
positivity, kindness, and compassion shines in her stories along
with her vulnerability, resilience, and courage that is refreshingly
showcased in her book. It has been a pleasure collaborating with
her on helping our mutual clients and 'patients' through difficult
times. Her advice on training and working in partnership with
your veterinary professional is spot on. Thank you, Laura for
sharing your unique experiences and insight!"

— **Dr. Jill Muraoka Lim, DVM,** founding
partner of Ohana Pet Hospital Ventura, CA

"Before meeting Laura, I could not imagine that animals had
much to say past wanting their people to understand why they
were behaving a certain way. However, I quickly learned that
animals are naturally connected to the Spirit World and to all of
the knowledge of the Universe. They can impart wisdom and

Truths generally expected from a very enlightened person. The nuggets of wisdom that the animals pass on to Laura can change the way we think about life, love, relationships, and more. I trust the words from animals more than I trust the words from some people, and after reading *Voices of the Animals,* you too will know, deep down, just how connected the animals are to the Source that moves through all things."

— **Kimberly Klein,** author of *Hummingbirds Don't Fly in the Rain* and *The Universe Speaks a Heavenly Dialogue*

The Conscious Bond™

# VOICES OF THE
# Animals

A collection of insightful articles and stories
that will change the way you view and treat animals.

## LAURA STINCHFIELD
### THE PET PSYCHIC®

The Conscious Bond™ Series
Voices of the Animals

Library of Congress Control Number: 2019915039
ISBN: 978-1-7333437-2-5 (print) • 978-1-7333437-3-2 (eBook)

Printed in the United States of America

Cover and Interior design: 1106 Design

Picture on front and back: Mitzi Mandel

Publisher's Cataloging-In-Publication Data
*(Prepared by The Donohue Group, Inc.)*

Names: Stinchfield, Laura, author.

Title: Voices of the animals : a collection of insightful
articles and stories that will change the way you view and
treat animals / Laura Stinchfield, the Pet Psychic®.

Other Titles: Conscious Bond

Description: Ojai, CA : The Pet Psychic®, [2019] | Series:
The Conscious Bond series ; [2] | A collection of articles and
stories many of which have been previously published.

Identifiers: ISBN 9781733343725 (print) | ISBN 9781733343732 (ebook)

Subjects: LCSH: Stinchfield, Laura--Career in animal
communication. | Human-animal communication. |
Animal communicators. | Animal behavior.

Classification: LCC QL776 .S752 2019 (print) | LCC
QL776 (ebook) | DDC 133.8/9--dc23

*This book is dedicated:*

*To my mom and dad, June and Grant Stinchfield,*
*for welcoming every animal I brought home into our family,*
*from parakeet to pony (except for the "smelly" ferret) and*
*for never telling me I was not talking with the animals.*

*To my brother Grant Stinchfield, who named me*
*"The Pet Psychic" in the '90s, and my sister, Zoë*
*Grave, who has always been one of my biggest fans.*

*And to my best friend, Kimberly Klein, for being a deep well*
*of support and for listening to all the strange happenings*
*in my life.*

# About Me, Laura Stinchfield — The Pet Psychic®

I have been a professional pet psychic/animal communicator since 1997, although I have been speaking with animals my whole life. My earliest memory is of my parents holding our Yorkshire terrier, Taffy, over my crib and having the feeling of her saying, "You are so small." It wasn't until my early 20s that I realized that I had an unusual ability (or super-power) and that not everyone could hear the animals.

From 1996 to around 2012, much of my business was animal training. I specialized in helping animals let go of their problem behaviors and become more confident, calm, and well-socialized pets. Becoming a full-time pet psychic evolved naturally. My years working as an animal trainer and Tellington-Touch practitioner helps every animal I speak with today.

I am grateful to be able to help thousands of animals and their people each year deal with and overcome behavioral and emotional issues. I am also grateful to be the trusted voice of the animals during illness, death, and dying, and for the ability to connect with animals in the afterlife and during their reincarnations.

I am blessed to be such a unifying part of the inner lives of animals and to have my work help so many.

I live in Ojai, California. My animal family includes Luca, my Poodle, Felix and Easter, my two Chihuahua mixes, Hudson, my white German Shepherd, Ella, my Snowshoe cat, Seamora, my Blue and Gold Macaw, Clyde, my Flemish Giant Rabbit, and Jubilee, my Appaloosa/Holsteiner horse.

# About this book

This book is a collection of articles and stories that were published from March 2018 through July 2019 with a bunch of edits and a few older articles thrown in.

The articles are about my life as a pet psychic and medium. Some of them are based on sessions I have had with clients and animals; others are interviews with my animals and those I've come across in my daily life. Other articles are written to educate my readers on animal behavior and body language, how to talk with animals, and how to support animals into becoming happier, healthier, and well-adjusted pets. Because I know many animal lovers are empathic beings, some of these articles I wrote to help my readers navigate their own feelings of overwhelming exhaustion, suffering, and compassion for others.

I feel you will find these articles and stories educational, entertaining, and enlightening. My intention is that they help you achieve a more conscious bond with the animals in your life and that they inspire you to open your eyes to the joys and miracles that are happening around you. Feel free to read this book with your pets. They will understand and enjoy it!

*"When you concentrate on your breathing and being positive, love is all around you. It is attracted to you. Love is what makes good beings have miracles."*

— QUOTE FROM MAIA, MY LATE WOLF-HYBRID, FEBRUARY 2, 2011

# Contents

# Chapter 1

# ANIMALS SPEAK

# My Life as a Pet Psychic
# The Conscious Bond™

I live my life as a pet psychic. It is really all I have ever known. My earliest memory is my parents holding our Yorkshire Terrier, Taffy, over my crib and hearing her say, "You are so small."

I hear the animals speaking to me in a whisper. This is telepathy. My mind transfers their thoughts, emotional feelings, and images in their heads into words. I can also feel their pain in my body. I have learned to quickly recognize what is my thought and my pain apart from what is someone else's. I know now how to let go of others' suffering, but I didn't always have this ability.

I do hear common themes from animals. Older animals pant and lick because they have acid reflux. Animals don't like to be left alone from daylight to dark without a light on in the house. To them, it feels as if they have been abandoned. They don't like two hands on their head at once. Would you? Cats like tall, wide water dishes so that their whiskers don't feel funny. They also like open windows looking out on active life at birdfeeders to stimulate them during the day. Dogs love big, green grassy parks and bodies of water, even if they don't like to swim. Common dying requests are bowls of ice cream, parties talking about how great they are, their people singing songs with their names in them, and eating their favorite meat. They know what makes us happy even if we have forgotten. They may tell someone who has not painted in twenty years to paint, leaving their owners speechless. Their animal wasn't even alive then. These owners write me months later to tell me they followed their animals' advice and that, not only do they have a more conscious bond with their pets, but everyone is happier all around.

Some of you may say, "I don't believe it." And I get that. I talk with animals and dead animals — and people, too! But if you have ever loved an animal, you may question your own judgment. Have animals ever comforted you when you were upset or initially disliked someone who eventually betrayed you? Have they surprised you by standing next to something you have lost or woken you up earlier when you forget to set the alarm? There is something in their eyes that says they understand. We have all seen it. Haven't you?

To make communication clearer, take a breath, and center yourself before you speak with them. Focus, but do not stare. Breathe rhythmically. Visualize everything that you say. If that is hard for you, be clear with your words. Tell the animals what you want rather than what you don't want. Instead of saying, "Don't jump," say, "Keep all four paws on the ground." You can tell them that when they jump, they may hurt someone by knocking them over, but when they keep all four paws on the ground, everyone is safe, and you are proud.

Whether we are conscious of it or not, our animals mirror us. Find peace in the moment. Take the time to use your eyes and watch them. Have they been misbehaving because you have been stressed? Do your animals' behaviors and emotional states change when you explain situations to them and how you would like them to act? If you begin to communicate more consciously with your pets, it's possible that your world may open up to a new understanding, and you just may experience the miracles of The Conscious Bond™.

# Pets Know More Than You Think

I am always fascinated by the consciousness of the animals that I speak with. Their thought process is often just as complex as some of the humans in my life. Some of the animals offer wise advice to their people. For instance, Marx, a big Newfoundland-type dog, said to his person (who, unbeknownst to me, had broken up with her boyfriend), "Healing takes time. Don't worry so much. The healing is happening. Sometimes, in the deep part of our soul, we have a longing, and that longing doesn't always match up with what we have in the world. When you experience a loss, the longing forces you to turn inward. When you look inside, you realize that you just need the sun to warm you a little bit. You need to get creative in your life to find the happiness and joy you deserve."

I told Marx that he was wise. I asked him what *he* longed for. He replied, "I am a wise guy. I do have a longing for snow and for running in the wilderness near snow." Marx has found happiness in the Santa Barbara, California, sun, but I bet his mom would take him on a road trip to see the snow.

A lean sable German Shepherd named Kali said about her person (mom), "I am not worried about my mom. She is super strong and can take care of herself. If she cries, she doesn't dwell on it, and she is back up and active. She is sort of like a super-mom. She does a lot, and I am proud of her for that. I don't think she realizes this, but my brain is just as smart as hers. I think that my mom needs to get new stationery and write letters to people she loves." Kali's person had been in a car crash and had been in recovery for months. She didn't necessarily feel like a "super-mom," but it was nice to hear. She purchased cards to write to her friends, because she felt that emails were impersonal and that people should go back to having pen pals. Kali could see that this was a healthy, positive act for her person, so she mentioned it.

Then there was Lola, a two-year-old Mastiff. Her person contacted me because she was getting aggressive with dogs in their apartment building and with the next-door neighbor's Golden Labrador. They shared a large patio. I explained to Lola that it was a positive thing that she had such a large patio. I explained that the Golden Lab's home opened up to the patio as well and that she needed to learn to share. I also explained that the other dog lived in a home like hers.

During our second session, Lola said, "I have to tell you something about myself. When you spoke to me last time, I thought to myself, *Why I am being so aggressive? Why am I letting my emotions take over my body?* Then I realized that I could just watch myself and then stop myself. I have been proud of myself, too. I think I had ideas in my mind that were not factual."

If I'm honest about it, I know that there are some people who do not have this kind of self-awareness and ability to change. But Lola had so much self-awareness, and her person had done her homework of explaining situations to Lola as well as implemented training advice. Lola's consciousness expanded even further, including a sense of purpose. During our third session, Lola said, "I feel like I could handle a job in which I trained to do lots of things, because I am feeling smarter than I have ever been. I feel like I have a purpose. I am not sure exactly what it is, but I know it's to be super well-behaved. I love it. It gives me a sense of greatness."

I wish more people were more like Lola. We should all strive for a sense of greatness and take accountability for our behavior. I am so proud of Lola's growth. Is it easier for a dog to get over itself than it is for a person? It's up to each individual to decide how much they want to change.

Here is a snippet from a testimonial that Lola's person wrote:

"We live in the city, and neighbors recently moved into the loft next door. They have a wonderfully friendly Golden Lab who also shares the patio with us. Naturally territorial, Lola didn't think he was so wonderful at first. She didn't understand the way that apartment buildings house multiple units, families, and dogs. She was already a handful when we would run into other dogs in the hallways, but her aggression on our shared patio took it to the next level. Lola would panic to get outside when she saw him on the patio. If we let her out, she would run at full speed to the barrier of planters, and try to lunge and growl in desperation toward his side of the patio. We spent much of our first call with Laura discussing the shared-space dynamic with Lola.

"After the call, I saw an immediate change in Lola's behavior. When I let her out on the patio that night, she didn't run over all anxious and stressful, trying to insert herself into the neighbor's area. Instead, she was cautious ... calmly inspecting their portion of the patio from afar. She continued to do so for the next few times I let her out that night and the next day.

"Lola mentioned in both follow-up calls that she has been talking to the dog next door and that they understand they have a special relationship with the shared patio. I noticed a significant change in the way Lola handles herself more calmly around dogs inside the building *and* outside the building, which used to be a challenge as well. Lola now responds calmly when I asks her to simply move on."

As you can see, our animals' consciousness are far more complex than is thought. Speak clearly to your animals about what you want from them. Develop clear boundaries and stimulate their minds with training. We are lucky to be able to share our lives with these intelligent beings. It is up to us to create the right environments for them to thrive in.

# A Glimpse into My Workweek

I talk with animals all day long. Here is a glimpse into each day of this past week.

On Tuesday, I spoke to Filson, a 14-year-old yellow Chow from Free Soil, Michigan. The first thing he said was, "You know, I have had an awesome life. I saw an eagle fly over my head. The smell of the wilderness is part of my soul. I got that from my mom. She embodies nature. I am very lucky in love."

Later in the session, he said, "This world is beautiful and awesome. Something created it. So, when I die, I am going to the place that created this world, so I am not worried."

The next day, his person sent me a video, taken the day before our session, of an eagle flying over Filson's head and the family dancing around Filson, singing "bird." It was a joyous memory for everyone.

Wednesday, a nine-year-old Pit Bull named Lovie from Fort Wayne, Indiana, told me, "My brain gets this really bad headache and my body quivers. I taste this terrible metallic taste in my mouth and I feel so sick. I feel terribly sick." They thought she was having GI issues, but she was actually having seizures. Now they know what to tell the veterinarian.

On Thursday, I spoke to a 15-year-old, cross-eyed cat named Sir Hamilton Crisscross from Baltimore, Maryland. He said, "I want my teeth cleaned because they feel gritty. I am not worried about going under because I am really healthy. My tooth hurts. It's infected up in there. I am going to live to be 25 years old, so I am still very young and agile. I may have strange eyes, but I can see perfectly fine. I think that we just need to go in there and have the doctor do his thing, and then, when I come out, do healing-energy work. It's when you pray for cats and their well-being. I know people who do this. Mom can find these people through a computer. There is this online community that can heal me so fast." Those people turned out to be his person's Facebook friends. I guess Sir Hamilton Crisscross has a fan club, and he knows it!

On Friday, I spoke with cat Vivian and her Yorkie brother Dashel. They are from Menlo Park, California. Dashel is new to the family and chases Vivian. She has some ideas to get him to stop. She says, "Can we do shock therapy on Dashel *(I told her no!),* or can we throw a towel over his head? I think that would annoy him." Dashel had his own ideas about Vivian. "Vivian likes to run. Does Vivian want to suckle on ears? I had a cat friend once that did that. We wrestled. I want a friend to wrestle with."

On Saturday, I spoke to a houseful of cats from Upstate New York. Hannah, an 18-month-old cat, said, "Dad says I am his princess favorite and that I should keep that a secret. He also told me that if I wanted to, I could go outside with him."

Her person told me that she overheard her husband telling Hannah that she is his princess and his favorite, but to keep it a secret. She also said he has been talking about building an outdoor cat enclosure connected to the house in the spring.

My horse, Jubilee, is in Bend, Oregon, where they are getting record amounts of snow. She told me today that Katie, her trainer, has been having emergency phone calls for most of the day. Turns out that Katie has been face-timing with her dad. They were troubleshooting because she was worried the snow was going to make the roof of the house and barn collapse.

# A Cat's Nightmare

It was late at night when I got a frantic email from a client: Hi, Laura. If you have a cancellation coming up soon, please, may I have it? My sweet little Bug viciously bit my forearm last night, let go, and then bit it again! It drew tremendous amounts of blood, and it is very painful. I know he's sorry, but I really would like to know what provoked him and make sure he knows that it was wrong. Very scary ... Thanks, Laura. Carol

Bug is a handsome white cat with big black patches on his body and a helmet-sized black patch over his head and ears. He is usually a very jolly cat. He once said to me about his person, "You know, when my mom is laughing, I want to bottle it up in one of those machines (meaning a cell phone) so that, when she is sad, she can listen to it again. Sometimes I try to make my mom laugh by moving my butt back and forth like a gigantic, fat dog. I think that is funny."

Biting his person is completely out of character for Bug. I have learned there are a number of reasons why animals bite out of the blue. It is usually either some type of pain in the body, like a pinched nerve or a post-traumatic-stress response, or there were signs all along, and the people just didn't see them. Signs people often miss are the animal's body getting stiff, staring, closing of the mouth, or squirming to get away. It is my job to ask Bug why he bit and what he was thinking and feeling when he did it.

Bug's person explained to me that it was an unusual night because she had friends over later than normal. Bug had been sitting on her lap, sleeping. The intense bites came immediately after she gently lifted him up and kissed him. This is something she does often with Bug. She stressed that he has never shown any aggression over the years. I believed her. She is a savvy, conscious pet owner.

It is unusual for an animal that does not normally bite to not only break the skin but to come back again for a second bite. I was eager to talk with Bug and to figure it out. I was worried about him and thought something must be seriously wrong.

What I heard from Bug was a big surprise to me.
Here is our conversation:

"What happened, Bug?" I asked.

Bug: "I don't understand something. I don't under-stand what happened! I was sleeping really peacefully, and, then, all of a sudden, I felt like there was a lake monster grabbing me. I bit the lake monster, and it roared at me — and then I bit it again!"

Me: "Bug, you bit your mom, and you bit her really bad. Do you understand? She lifted you up to kiss you, and you bit her."

Bug: "Umm …. my mom is the lake monster? She *touched* me? *No!* The lake monster grabbed me! Seriously grabbed me!"

Me: "It must have been a dream. Do you think you were dreaming?"

Bug: "No, it couldn't have been a dream because my mom came and chased the lake monster away! No way that I bit my mom! That wasn't the lake monster?" He was clearly upset and confused.

I couldn't grasp that he actually thought there was a lake monster that bit him. Where would he come up with that? I wanted to get more information before I told my client what he said. I wasn't satisfied with his answer. So, I continued to ask him questions.

Me: "Do you have any pain in your body?"

Bug: "In my body? Pain? No, I am a super-good jumper. No, I don't have pain right now. I am sort of exhausted from the last couple of days because we wrangled that lake monster. It was overwhelming."

Now, that was it. I was going to have to tell his person that he thought she was a lake monster. This was one of those times I wished I had heard something different. It happens all the time, actually. The animals say something that is so out of the ordinary that it worries me that the client can't make sense of it. Thank goodness she is a regular client and understands that it may take some thinking before some things make sense.

To my surprise, it made complete sense to her immediately! "I know exactly what that is!" she exclaimed. She then told me that they live on a lake. A few days earlier, Bug had followed her down to the lake and onto the dock while she was feeding the ducks at which time catfish always like to join in the feast. A huge catfish jumped up toward him, twisted in the air, and splashed back into the water. Bug got drenched, freaked out, and ran off the dock and back up to the house.

He is now terrified of the catfish, also known as "the lake monster." Bug had a nightmare. When I explained to him what had happened, he said, "I feel terrible now. Do tell my mom I am sorry."

Still frightened, he said, "That animal came through dimensions into my dreams! Because I can talk with you, I think anything can happen. Anything at all ... Do catfishes eat cats? Tell me the truth. How is it possible to live underwater? Can you tell him to move?"

There is never a day that I am not amazed at the deep, complex consciousness of our pets. I agree with Bug. Anything can happen. Anything at all.

# If I Tell the Truth,
# They Might Get Rid of Me

Because animals are so pure at heart and live in the present moment, I was in awe when I learned that some of them can lie. What would be their purpose for lying?

Just last week, Graham, a one-year-old Border collie/Great Pyrenees mix adamantly told me that he was not the one who had chewn the irrigation lines. I had discussed this issue with him several times prior. When the ranch hand caught him in the act once again, we needed to have another discussion. Graham told me, "It was not me. It must have been a gopher." He also lied and told me that he'd eaten *one* goose egg — not the *six* that he had been seen stealing out of the nests.

Why does Graham feel the need to lie? I originally thought it was a complex, thought-out behavior, but maybe it's just an instinctual self-preservation behavior. When I pressed Graham more about his lying, he said, "If I tell the truth, they might get rid of me. Sometimes I do those behaviors because it feels like the right thing to do in the moment (just being a puppy). But then they are so mad at me that they threaten they will give me away. I don't want to leave this home. I am happy here." Oh, the amount of stress we put on animals when we flippantly tell them something that might not even be true. Can you imagine a one-year-old rescue dog worried that his person's threats of giving him away are real? Does it keep him up at night? Does it contribute to more chewing behaviors? Those are the things we must ask ourselves when we say things we think they don't understand.

Then there is Millie, a beautiful, middle-aged calico cat. She walks like a ballerina and takes great care to keep herself impeccably groomed. She is extremely neat in the litter box. She lives with several other cats and two dogs. Her brother cat, Jack, is a big, friendly male who often brings his kills into the house and makes a mess with the litter. He has been known to poop outside the litter box from time to time.

Recently, one of the cats was often peeing outside the litter box, but the people were unable to catch them in the act. They didn't know who it was. Millie blames it on Jack. She says with confidence that she has seen him do it. It's believable because Jack has been known for making messes, but Jack blames it on Millie. Who is telling the truth? The other animals either say they don't know, or they blame it on Millie. "No way," their people say. "Millie is our perfect cat. She would never do that. It has to be Jack."

Cameras were set up, and Millie was caught in the act. "Why are you peeing, and why are you lying?" I asked her.

Millie answered, "My dad does it to my mom all the time. He tells her he is one place, but he is somewhere else. I am pissed off at him, and I felt like if I lied, my mom might be able to see that someone she thinks is perfect can also do bad things when they want to. I wanted to show my mom how bad my dad was being. I didn't feel like I should tell my dad's secrets. I felt like he should tell my mom."

Wait — what? Did Millie just understand that her dad is cheating on her mom and, by peeing outside the litter box and lying about it, she is showing her mom that the perfect one can be up to no good? Once Millie explained her reasoning, she stopped peeing outside the box. I don't know what happened between her mom and her dad.

So, Graham lied because he was scared of losing his home, and Millie lied because she felt uncomfortable telling her person's secrets. Our behavior and what we say and feel around our animals impact not only their behavior but also their state of mind. The more we strive for honest communication and right behavior, the better the welfare of our animals. We are all connected. When there is an issue, we must look at the whole.

# Animals' Intuition Can Be Life-Saving

In 2012, a woman called me from France to speak with her two elderly dogs. Prior to our session, I always have my clients fill out a form. For Babette, a 12-year-old black-grayish Poodle mix dog, the client had written, "She is losing her bounce and may be losing accurate sight. Always hungry, likes sleeping on or in beds. A bit bossy, very faithful!!!"

The questions for Babette were, "Are you happy? Is anything troubling you — especially pain? How long do you want to stay alive?"

The other dog was Milou, a 12-year-old ginger-and-white, long-haired Husky-looking dog. His person wrote about him, "He has an irregular heartbeat and pain in his spine. He is growing old quickly." My client's questions for Milou were, "When do you want to go? How much pain are you in? Do you know I appreciate your love and support?"

This is a typical older-dog questionnaire. I have sessions like this many times a week. The animals usually discuss their wants and needs, beds they would like, or the type of diet and supplements that make them feel better or worse. I ask where and how bad their pain is; how much they love their people; things they want to do and/or places they want to go. Dying is often discussed.

Babette and Milou surprised me. They talked about these things, but they also kept bringing up a young four-year-old boy who turned out to be my client's grandson, Adam. They were very concerned about him. His parents were divorced, and, at the time, he lived part-time with his Grandma and his father and part-time with his mother.

Babette said, "I want to tell my mom that I am so thankful for her. I am really happy. The cold chills my bones, and I have a hard time moving. The right side of my neck gets stiff. I have tingling down to my right paw. I feel a weird feeling in my throat. I still love life. I would love to go for a longer walk every day. Mom needs to get a break from work.

"Something is troubling me about Adam. I feel like he needs my mom to take care of him more. My mom really understands him. My mom has a way of talking to all of us. I think he needs my mom to talk to him. Mom, when you talk to him, know that he doesn't need to be looking at you to be listening. He listens to you all the time even if he is focused away from you."

Milou said, "Well, I have to tell my mom that I am very worried about Adam, too. I lose sleep over it. I think that his mother is not listening to him at all and screaming at him. It makes him scared to talk. Our mom should be his mom. When he is here, he looks different. He trusts our mom. He doesn't trust his mom. Mom, I know it is really hard for you, but I want you to talk to him. He never had anyone tell him how amazing he is. He needs someone to tell him how amazing he is.

"Yes, I am in pain. I have pain behind my eyes and in my hips. I feel nauseous a lot of the time. I feel really sick. I feel like I am falling apart. My stomach cramps a lot. My back is sore. I am not ready to die yet. Can you sit outside with me? Mom, when I die, are you going to help me? Are you going to be there with me?"

Then, all of sudden, I heard the cat in the family. Bombay said, "Mom, I am trying to tell you something. We are sick about Adam, and we just don't know what to do about him. We feel like this is so important. His mom may be abusing him in some way. Mom, this is serious."

Then Adam's young pit bull dog, Mack, joined in. "All this talk about Adam is making me nervous. We need to figure this out quickly. Grandma, you are so cool. You undergo hardships so that we all have a safe place. I'm grateful."

It can be an uncomfortable situation for me when the client wants to talk about one subject, but the animals keep talking about another very personal and serious matter. I never know how people are going to take it. I left this phone call very sad for Adam.

It was not until six years later, in June of 2018, that I heard what happened after this call. This client booked a session again to talk about a rescue dog she'd recently adopted. She thanked me for our previous session and told me that, after our session, she'd done some investigating. She found that Adam's mother was, in fact, abusing him and also drugging him so that he would have less energy at home. My client went to social services, and the result was that she and her son got full custody of Adam.

These animals changed Adam's life and got him out of harm's way! Our animals' consciousness never ceases to amaze me. Doesn't this make you want to look at your animals and wonder, *What do you know and understand? Is it something that I don't know?*

# When Your Dog
# Hates Your Boyfriend

I am being interviewed for an article on my work for a fashion magazine, on the patio of a small cottage that overlooks the Malibu coast. My interviewer, Amy, oddly shuffles for a second in her chair and runs her fingers through her hair. I wonder, *What has bothered her? She is confident, and her questions show genuine interest in my work.*

Amy is in her early 30s, with perfectly brushed hair — the kind of hair I will never have. Mine is always wild, as if I have been out on galloping horses, but hers is perfect, with not a strand out of place. I am jealous of that. She gets up and walks over to her dog, Charlie, a cocker spaniel whose blond fur has an uncanny resemblance to his person's hair.

Amy bends down to stroke him, turns to me with eyes as big as Charlie's, and asks me, "Will you ask him what has been bothering him lately? He is not as happy as he used to be. I am worried he is sick. Like dying sick. Something is off — I know it."

"Of course," I reply.

She stands up and taps her side. Charlie rises, and, in unison, side by side, they head toward where I am sitting.

I smile at the sound of Amy's heels and Charlie's nails on the tile patio.

"What's wrong, Charlie?" I ask. "Your mom feels like maybe something's wrong. How does your body feel?"

Charlie lays his head in my lap and looks sadly up into my eyes. I pet his head. His fur feels soft and healthy. "I feel fine," he says with a sigh.

"Then what is wrong?" I ask.

Charlie replies, "I hate my mom's boyfriend. We do fun things. We go to the beach and out to eat, and I can sleep in the bed, but he does little mean things that make her unhappy. She's been happier than she is now. She doesn't dance around the house anymore. She is sad sometimes, wondering where he is or what he has been doing. I don't want her to marry him. He is not good for her. I am worried he is going to make her sick."

I am about to relay this message to Amy when Charlie nudges my arm and says, "I want my mom to have a man who makes her feel safe. Who adores her as much as mom adores me. I want her to have the feeling that we have. The feeling that she will always be loved and treasured and without secrets that hurt my mom's energy and happiness. I want my mom to thrive in life, not get sick."

As I relay the message to Amy, tears stream out of her eyes. "So, Charlie is not sick?"

"It doesn't seem like it," I reply.

"I feel like my boyfriend is going to ask me to marry him soon," she says with a half-smile and tilt of her head in contemplation.

I say, "It doesn't sound like Charlie is jealous of him. Charlie showed me there is a nice, charming side to him. Is there any truth in the other side of your boyfriend that Charlie mentions?"

I ask this for two reasons. One to get the bottom of what is going on with Charlie and figure out how to get him out of his funk. The other reason is for girl power. The thought of charming, secretive men who slowly chip away at women's self-esteem makes me unsettled. Everyone deserves to be in a relationship that offers an honest sense of safety, fun, and the feeling of being loved and treasured. If Charlie's assessment is true, it could save years of unhappiness in Amy's life.

*She is a strong woman,* I think, as I watch Amy wipe her eyes with a tissue, take a long drink of lemon water, and then call Charlie to her. He trots over to her with his tail wagging and his head erect. She kneels down to him and gives him a big hug and smile. *I heard you, Charlie. I'll think about what you said.*

A few weeks later, there is a nice article about me in the fashion magazine, with no mention of my talk with Charlie.

Six months later, I get an email. "Laura, I can't thank you enough. I listened to Charlie and broke up with my boyfriend. He begged me to stay and get married. All I could think was *Charlie doesn't like you.* I have since met the most amazing man. I am back to dancing with Charlie in the kitchen. I feel safe and treasured, and you will be happy to hear Charlie is back to his playful self!"

# Answers to Dilemmas May Come in Unexpected Ways

My first client of the day was Bruce, a local small terrier-mix and his person. Bruce has had significant body issues ever since he was young.

Bruce starts out the session saying, "I have so much to say. My body is having tremors. In my dreams, I run really fast, so you don't need to worry about me. I do get some running in. When I am awake, I can feel very much alive. Since the chiropractor, I wag my tail better and move my head lower, but I definitely have been having some strange tremors that worry me."

Then he goes on to say, "I feel that there needs to be a shift in consciousness of all animals and people. We need to stand solid on the ground and have a vision of what we want. Sometimes I feel like there is a mountain of possibilities, but I am only seeing one. I want to manifest something else in my life, but I am having trouble with it. I think I need massage time, just sitting and visualizing what I want to be. I want more movement. You know what else I was thinking about? My mom and I could go to do that needle medicine (acupuncture). I know that would strengthen me."

We went on to talk about a few more things, and then suddenly Bruce offers dating advice: "If anyone ever tells you that they love you and you believe them, and then they go off and tell other people that they love them, too, you should just be like, 'I don't know if I love you' and then walk away. You should do this to see if they dance like birds do to get your attention. If he truly loves you, then when those others come near him, he will chase them away. He will chase them away because he has set himself on only one bird, and that is you. I feel that should be known."

We couldn't figure out why Bruce was offering this advice. It didn't ring true for his person. I told her to keep it in the back of her mind because perhaps it will make sense in the future.

My next appointment was a Maltese named Chewy, who lives across the country. Chewy also has significant body issues. He starts the session with, "Sometimes I don't sleep with my mom (person) at night because I am getting a cramping in my butt area, and, when we bump into each other, it hurts." He goes on to talk about other pains like his stomach and tingling down his spine.

Then he offers, "I love my mom's sweet songs and lying in the sunlight. I love our outings. I am still very active and happy. I feel like I want that medicine that comes in a shot/needle form (acupuncture) that you just spoke to the other dog about, and I want one of those massages, too."

My heart filled with amazement. Sweet little Chewy had been listening to my last session. I had an eavesdropper, and I didn't even know it! His person told me that she had been telling him that I was going to call, to pay attention, and to be ready. Well, he certainly was!

I thought for a moment and then did something I have never done before. I asked Chewy's person to listen to Bruce's (another client's!) dating advice to see if it applied to her. After I read it, there was a gasp on the phone. "A dog said that?! Yes, that applies to me. I just told a guy yesterday that he is disrespecting me by leading other women on. Now I know what to do!"

There is always an answer to our dilemmas. Trust and be aware that it may arrive in unexpected ways.

# Leave It to a Cat

I had a phone session with a woman named Karen. She had a seven-year-old female calico cat, named Audrey, who had big golden eyes. Karen wanted to know if there was anything Audrey wanted to say or anything she wanted or needed.

Audrey started the conversation with, "My mom has gone through a lot in the last few years. Her heart is opening up like a spring flower. You know music when it sounds like doom-thunder time, and then it gets relaxed? Mom is in the relaxed stage." Karen shared that she'd recently gone through a bad breakup. During this time, there had been a lot of thunderstorms and flooding in her state, which is where "doom thunder" came from.

Audrey went on to talk about wanting her water dish scrubbed more often, a different type of litter, and to go outside at night so she could see "the amazing stars in the sky." "I am really enjoying the new bathroom smell. It would be nice if that was in the living room," she said. Turns out her mom had recently put a new fragrant soap in the bathroom.

Audrey continued, "There is this one peachy-colored facial cream that looks extraordinary on my mom." Karen had been diligent about taking care of her skin lately. Audrey was clearly using the session to give her mom an emotional pep talk.

When I asked Audrey if she missed her old dad, she replied, "Oh, my goodness. I will tell you a thing about him. He is sort of like a TV. The conversation goes one way, not two ways. You talk to him, and sometimes you get nothing back. Even I respond better. I would go to him and be like, 'Are you in there?' He is not an emotionally stable guy. I feel bad for him because he has some type of hiccup in his head. I don't need to see him again. He is not mom-worthy."

Karen shared that her ex-boyfriend was not very communicative or empathetic to her feelings. Time and time again, animals will tell their people through me that their significant other or their ex does not treat them right or is not the right person for them. In these situations, it's always a little awkward to be the animal's translator, but it is also an honor.

When the truth is spoken so practically, a still moment follows in which the client gets very quiet. I wait it out, because deep change is occurring. The people are processing their animal's level of consciousness and the reality of what was just said. They realize that all the trauma they went through, where they thought that they were all alone, there was actually a silent observer who witnessed, understood, and cared for them the whole time. Their animal was not just there to snuggle with them, but also understood the complexity of the situation and had compassion for their plight. It's a "Whoa! Ah, ha!" moment that excites me because I know that animal will be looked at differently from that moment forward. This doesn't just happen with breakups; it can happen with illness, work issues, and conflict in any relationship. The animals are super aware.

When I am listening to the animals, sometimes I chuckle too loudly to myself and then have to pull it together while I translate what was said. Like when Audrey goes on to give her mom dating advice: "Mom, just be yourself, and know that you have awesomeness inside of you. If you have to *ask* yourself, 'Does this guy know I am awesome?' Get rid of him before he breaks your heart. Also wear cool shoes, so when you kick him out of the house, you can think about your cool shoes rather than the disappointing guy."

Leave it to a cat to give the best advice.

## Chapter 2

# TALKING WITH AND UNDERSTANDING THE ANIMALS

# Calming Signals — Learning Your Animal's Behavior

In the 1990s, the Norwegian dog trainer and behaviorist, Turid Rugaas, studied canine behavior, and in 1996 published the widely acclaimed book *On Talking Terms with Dogs: Calming Signals.* Turid teaches how to be a keen observer of canine behavior. I would not be half the animal person I am today without the knowledge and study of her work. We can use Turid's work to understand the behaviors of many species.

Animals' number-one form of communication is body language. We want them to understand our verbal cues first and foremost, but that is unfair to them. It is up to us to learn their body language so that we can efficiently teach them our verbal one. Animals use body language to calm themselves or other animals in stressful situations, to show dominance or submission, to communicate to us where they have pain in their body, or to show us when they are confused or confident. Some of these body-language signals are looking away, blinking, yawning, fake-sniffing the ground, approaching in an arc, shaking (looks similar to dogs shaking off water), sitting, lying down, and play-bowing.

Body signals of lack of calming or when an animal is getting stressed are: Closing/clenching of the mouth, staring, leaning on the front paws, body and tail getting stiff, and panting. These often lead to fear or territorial aggression or timid behaviors, or even fooling-around behaviors like young dogs running around spastically.

It can be dangerous not to know and understand these signals. Most humans expect domesticated animals to learn human voice commands and hand signals without acknowledging that animals have a native language of their own. This is selfish on our part. Often when people do not understand animal body language, they inadvertently are late to discipline or scold an animal at the time of inappropriate behavior and may scold while the animal is calming itself. This can result in increased aggression, fear, lack of confidence, and illness, and, in general, it creates confusion and dysfunction in the animals' lives. We often see this with shock-collar, prong, and pinch-collar use. The handler is late to shock or correct and ends up correcting during a calming signal. This teaches a dog it is unsafe to calm itself. Wait — did you get that? Let me repeat it: Bad timing of corrections can teach our dogs that it is unsafe to calm themselves. If you are an average human, you probably have bad timing. Think about that for a moment.

People call me and wonder why their dog is getting increasingly stressed and aggressive over time when they are putting in so much time and money into training. Handlers are damaging the instinctual nature of peace in our dogs and forcing them to reach higher levels of stress.

But it's not just in corrections that we can be confusing to our animals.

It is important to pay attention to our own body language and how we may be sending an animal a mixed message. For instance, a human may think bending over with one's torso to greet an animal is welcoming, when, in actuality, it is telling an animal that you are more dominant and that they must submit to you. You may notice this when dogs are dominant to one another (in play or aggression). One may throw a chin or paw up on the other one's shoulder, or you may notice this when you are asking your dog to come to you. They may stop a few feet away and watch you, wanting to be respectful and not come underneath you.

If you call your dog too loudly and dominantly with firm eye contact, your dog may start to fake-sniff or come to you in an arc, asking you to please calm your voice and body language, letting you know with their language that they mean no harm. But people misread this and label their dogs "stubborn" or say their dogs are ignoring them when neither is true. They are communicating with you the only way they know how. If you want an animal to feel safe and come to you, bend with your knees, not with your torso, and/or blink your eyes or turn your body to the side. This concept is the reason that, when you turn and walk or run in the opposite direction, your dog is right at your heels. You are safer to approach, and, by turning away, you are communicating to your dog that you mean no harm to them.

Another common misconception is thinking it is disrespectful if the animal looks at you and then looks away when you are speaking with them. Holding eye contact is also a form of dominance in the animal kingdom. Your animal is being polite when they look and look away. You may also see these behaviors in children when you are disciplining them. These calming language signals are instinctual across species. Pay attention to when you yawn.

If we start to mindfully watch the animals, we can praise an animal for exhibiting calming signals which will, in turn, build confidence, independence, and communication skills in all situations and relationships. For instance, if you have two animals that are not getting along in the house, you can start praising them for the positive communication skills. The dog is staring at the cat with his mouth closed and then looks away — praise. The cat licks or fake-grooms in the presence of the dog — praise. We can also teach the animals to look away when we see them staring at each other and then praise. This will remind them how to calm themselves. We can do this during any stressful situation. When in doubt, teach an animal to retreat from what makes them nervous or to go behind you for safety.

We should start to notice an animal's behavior as we approach them or are petting them. If their eyes start to stare, their mouth closes, and their body gets stiff, we should retreat. Perhaps the animal is nervous and may bite, or perhaps we have just touched a sore spot on the animal's body. In general, a soft eye and open mouth is safe.

If people use their knowledge of animal behavior to communicate more efficiently with their animals, it will build their animals' confidence and trust. The bond between human and animal will become more affectionate and understanding. Start watching your animals more closely, and see what you discover.

# Preparing Your Animals
## for a Trip to the Vet

My animals have never had a problem going to the vet. Sure, it's not their favorite thing to do, but they stay calm and attentive. They don't exhibit high levels of stress by panting, barking, or meowing. They don't shake or stiffen their body. They don't refuse to go into the vet clinic or snap or bite while we are in there. Well, maybe Felix, my Chihuahua, will snap a bit while being handled, but he does it more to communicate than because he is stressed, and it's still easy to work with him.

Let's face it: Veterinary hospitals are scary places. They have a strong, sterile smell. Other animals are fearful. People do things to the animals that are unnatural and against animal instincts. Without realizing it, people are exhibiting dominant or somewhat aggressive behaviors by leaning over the animals evaluating them, staring into their eyes, and palpating their abdomen. They put cold things up against the animals' hearts and make strange faces while doing it. They stick something up their butt or swab their sensitive ears. They poke animals with needles that can make the animals feel pretty yucky for some time.

So, how do we make these visits better for our pets? If you have an animal who travels well, bring them to the vet clinic just for a visit. Let the staff give them treats and some happy, welcoming pets and faces. But also, you can talk with the animals. Explain to them what the vet is all about. Take a breath. Clear your thoughts, and, with a clear, detailed explanation, tell your pet that a visit to the vet's office is to keep them healthy. A stick up their butt is to read their body temperature. Something cold held to their body is to hear the beat of their heart to make sure it has a healthy rhythm. A light in the eyes is to check to see how well they are seeing. A needle is to pull blood to test how all their organs are working or to give them a shot to keep them healthy. A needle in their bladder is to see if they have an infection. A palpating of the abdomen is to check for an abnormal tumor. If they are at the vet's because they are sick, tell them the doctor is trying to find out why they are throwing up or having seizures or whatever their ailment is. Tell your animal that you know the people act strangely, but that it's to help them live longer. Tell your animal if they have pain anywhere to tell the vet in their mind over and over and to physically exaggerate the pain to let the vet know. If you are in the examining room with your animal, you can explain what is happening and why in real time. You can do this out loud, or you can do it in your head, sending it to your pet's heart center.

Remind your animals how to calm themselves. Tell them to lick, yawn, stretch, blink their eyes, and breathe. Remind them they are OK. Tell them you like your vet and you trust them. Remind your animal they will be going home with you. Whatever diagnoses or news you hear, be sure to tell your animal either at the vet's office or when you get home. Talk to your vet about something personal. What animals do they have? What do they like to do in their free time? Make them a real person instead of someone who is just poking and prodding your animal. Your animal is listening to everything you say. It's up to you to be calm enough so they can understand.

If it's appropriate, touch your animal. Learn the Tellington-Touch, rub their ears, or just stroke your animal in slow, rhythmic, connective strokes. The calmer your touch, the calmer your pet. Make sure you touch them consciously and not in a fast and nervous way that reflects your feelings. This is not the time for your animal to be your therapy animal. *You* need to be there for *them*. Pull it together. Know that it is OK.

Even if the visit becomes chaotic, stay positive. If you are nervous, your animal will be nervous. Sometimes your animal's relationship to the vet's office is all about your attitude. Choose a safe and confident attitude, and your animal will learn to deal with it — and maybe even enjoy it. My animals love to see their vets. Find a vet you love and trust no matter what it takes. Do this while your animals are healthy so that, when they get sick, you and your animal feel taken care of and that your vet's advice is the right thing to listen to.

# How to Prepare Your Animal for Surgery

Whether it is a teeth-cleaning, spay/neuter, or a major surgery of removing a tumor or fixing a knee, having our animals go under anesthesia can be a scary thing — though it doesn't have to be. The number-one priority is to use a veterinarian you trust. If you feel uneasy about your vet, find someone else. If anything ever goes wrong, you want to feel confident that the veterinarian will make smart decisions. In my business, I do hear the horror stories of the animals dying on the table or hours after surgery, but they are rare, and, when they do happen, there is a greater plan involved. It was the animal's time to go, and/or as nightmarish as it may sound, there were lessons to be learned.

Peace, confidence, and knowledge are powerful elements that we can instill in our pets before their surgery. If you have decided that your animal must have surgery, then you have the feeling it is the "right" thing. Surrender to the "right" thing, and find peace with it. Find that still place within your core, and radiate it out with confidence to your pet. Talk with your pet. Tell them that they will be going to the veterinarian. Explain what they are going to do and why. Tell them that they are going to be given medicine to make them fall asleep. They may feel groggy. Tell them to be brave, and know that they will be OK. Tell them their teeth are going to be cleaned, that they are going to get neutered, so they cannot make babies, that their knee is going to be fixed, or that a tumor is going to be removed to see if we can get them to live a longer life. Tell them that they may wake up with a headache, feel nauseous, that the lighting on the cages may be strange, that they may be sore in the area they were operated on. Tell them that those feelings are normal and that they will feel better soon. Tell them that, when they are asleep, they may have good dreams in which they see their friends. Tell them that there are angels or beings of light who are watching over them and protecting them. Tell them that you love them and that there is a cord of love connecting you both so that you will always be close. Tell them when they will be picked up from their surgery — that night or in a couple of days. Tell them that the doctors will take good care of them and that you trust their doctor. Tell your pet with a smile that they are brave and are going to do great.

Once the surgery is over and you pick them up, if they are in the room with you, try to remain calm. Because of the drugs, they are going to be groggy, so you don't want to seem too emotional. It will confuse them. They will hear and understand bits and pieces of what the vet is telling you. It's important to explain this to them later. Once they are home and stable, tell them what the recovery will look like. Will they have to be contained or wear a cone? Will their exercise be limited? Will they need medicine? Tell them everything you know. Don't keep secrets. They will know it. Explain to them what the doctor found. Be positive. Believe in health. This is extremely important. Believe in your animal's ability to heal themselves. Tell them they will feel better. Be calm, focus on the positive, and know that the right way for both of you will reveal itself. When you connect yourself to the loving force field of health and well-being, everything will fall into place. If you find yourself starting to panic, come back to your breath, and settle into the love you feel for your pet. See if you can find peace and strength at your core. There is a deep love that resides within all of us. It is from that place that all is healed and understood. The animals know this. Guide them to it, and experience the greater bond.

# Planning a Move?
# How to Ease the Stress
# of Your Pet

Moving can be stressful for you and your pets. Watching the home get packed up into boxes can give animals stomach upset or an onset of behavioral problems. Your animal may take on your worries. Cats may lick themselves raw and dogs may become destructive. But this does not have to be. When I was in my 20s, I moved often with a dog and a cat. I was thrilled with the adventure of it, and so my animals were, too. They traveled easily and could acclimate to any new home, friend's house, or hotel room. I did not worry, so neither did they. There is power in your intention and beliefs. At that time in my life, it was not in my consciousness that my animals would not be OK. When I left them alone in strange places, it was just our life, and I figured they would go with the flow. Therefore, my animals were always happy and well adjusted. I have found that if my clients make a conscious effort to be OK with the move and believe that their animals will be OK, too, even the most worrisome of pets will surprise you with their calm demeanor.

Knowledge is power. Tell your animal what to expect. Tell them how long you will be packing up the house, what the trip will look and feel like, and what the new home will be like. Be excited for your life change. Try to keep their routine the same, even when traveling. Feed and exercise them at the same time of day. Have some items from home available to them, such as special blankets or toys and/or their regular food dishes. If there is going to be something chaotic, tell them. Driving at night? Tell them there will be lights outside the car window. Flying on a plane? Explain to them about the crowded airport, noises, and the change in pressure of the cabin.

I have spoken to hundreds of animals to prepare them to travel to other countries and who have had to endure an overnight layover or a quarantine on the other side. All of these animals, even the elderly ones, arrived without getting sick or traumatized because I told them about everything — the conveyor belts; the wind and noise on the tarmac; the crates moved with little care; the intense smells; the people who speak a different language; how many times they will be in and out of an airplane; how long they will be at the kennel or in quarantine; how they may or may not get their regular food; how it's important, if they have to go to the bathroom, to go inside their crates in the corner and not to worry about it (their people will clean them on the other side); how important it is to eat and drink when they are offered food and water; how it's important to stay near their crate even if something happens and the crate falls apart and it's loud and scary. I tell them to freeze and not to run, and to trust people even if they look scary.

There is strength in telling others what to expect. Some people want to hide the chaos and keep it a secret, thinking they are protecting others, but that is not so. The more they know how to be prepared, the easier it will be for them. If none of the chaos materializes, they will feel they had a pretty easy trip.

Once you get to your destination, make sure your animals have a safe spot to hang out in and call their own. Put their bed in a corner with their toys or special blanket. Put their food and water near their bed. Keep their area small at first while you unpack and get your things settled.

Tell them this is their new home. Be excited. Be happy for your new beginning. The happier you are, the safer your pets will feel.

# Oh, Baby!

Having a baby in the house with animals can be a hard adjustment for some pets. The high-pitched screams, the stinky diapers, and the change in the home routine and walk schedule can be confusing. Animals may act out by becoming more destructive, barking or meowing more, and/or — God forbid — aggressive to the baby. The good news is that, if you prepare your pet for the new addition into the house, this situation can be a positive one.

This family with three dogs spent the time to prepare their dogs. Before the baby came, we had an extensive conversation explaining to them every aspect of the wonder — *and* chaos — that living with the new addition could bring.

Here is what some animals say about two and a half months after the baby comes home. Doogie is a seven-year-old, brindle-colored Shepherd mix with floppy ears, gray around the muzzle, and large, sensitive eyes. His person is most concerned about Doogie around the baby because he is "the most dominant and demanding dog in the house." When I asked Doogie how he feels about his new human brother and why he constantly wants to be around the baby, he answered, "He is just as much mine as he is yours. It's a dangerous house for babies. I need to make sure he is protected and that he is safe. Listen — I never knew there could be such an amazing character in a body that blows bubbles. I don't want to miss anything."

Doogie's people were so relieved that he sees their son as a part of the family and that he is excited about the experience. Doogie is mirroring how the people feel about their addition. It's so important to watch your thoughts and feelings around your animals and to be careful not to project your fears around them.

Chelsea is a beautiful white dog with brown patches around her eyes, ears, and torso. She looks like a small Akita with short fur. Before the baby came, she said, "I feel a bit worried about the baby coming. I feel the baby is going to be a bit of — how do I say this — a *nuisance* at first. When my people tell others, 'We are having a baby,' everyone gives us a look that says, 'Oh, man — that is a lot of work,' and I think, *Why are they not getting excited?*"

I told her I thought it would be fun, and she answered, "You think it will be fun? Can the baby play tug?"

Two and a half months after the baby was born, Chelsea said, "Our baby is going to be awesome to play with. Sometimes I see our baby's spirit flying around the room, laughing, and dancing. He is a big rainbow colored light. He is a happy baby. I need to smell his feet every day. I also want couch time right next to them. If you ever need a babysitter, I can do it. I am definitely more chill. That is what you need with him. When you fuss, he gets fussier, but if you chill with him, he goes into silence. I know how to do it. You gently stroke his head into sleeping, and then you tiptoe away."

Ginny, a three-year-old brindle colored dog who looks like a Labrador-Weimaraner mix, is a little more concerned about the baby than the other dogs. She says, "I want to know why the baby has such a loud voice sometimes. Why doesn't the baby crawl? Does the baby know that I am here? He doesn't recognize me. That makes me sad. I think his lower back hurts. Why does mom pat him on the back so much? Do you think that the baby will get to know us better?"

When you treat your animals as if they are conscious beings, they begin to understand life on a deeper level. Just like humans, they have different personalities and different ways of looking at each situation. If you take the time to be observant, you will know when they have questions. Take a leap of faith, and answer them.

# Juliette — How to Tell Your Animal You Are Going Away

I always knew what animals were thinking and feeling, but it wasn't until I was twenty-one years old that I realized animals could understand me. My cat Juliette taught me this. I rescued Juliette when my Shepherd/Coyote dog, Lala, lay by Juliette's cage and refused to leave the pet store. Lala was known to do this with rocks she became obsessed with on trails, but never with another animal. Impulsively, I filled out an application for Juliette, which got instantly accepted. This would never happen today for a young woman in a rental. I left the pet store with a bag each of dog and cat food, a litter box, and a cardboard box with Juliette in it. I knew nothing about acclimating a cat to a new house so when I got home, I just let her out of the box with the doors of the house wide open. Juliette fit right in like she'd lived there all along.

Juliette was a beautiful, small, tan colored cat. Her dainty white paws turned outward slightly, which made her walk like a ballerina. I often found her and Lala snuggled up together on the couch or outside under one of the maple trees. Juliette would follow us across the lane to Peach Lake and jump into the canoe with my boyfriend, Lala, and me, and go rowing around the lake. She often accompanied us on long walks around the golf course, dashing ahead of us and up trees, or climbing on top of boulders with Lala in tow.

My boyfriend, Evan, Lala, and I often went backpacking or would spend the night out on their family yacht on the Long Island Sound. Then, I never thought about bringing Juliette, but today, I would. While we were gone, my sister would stop by daily to check on Juliette. Juliette was supposedly fine while we were gone, but when we would return, she was clearly very angry. She would wait for us on the front stoop and rub up against Lala, but she wouldn't let me pet her. She'd give me a scolding look and then dash out of the yard. She would be gone one or two nights. I was always very worried, waking up in the middle of the night to call her. Even Lala would search for her, to no avail. When Juliette decided to come home, she wouldn't look at me all day and night. She was never a cuddly cat, but she loved to be around us and had soulful, expressive eyes. It was heartbreaking to see her in such distress.

I found a book called *Animal Talk*, by Penelope Smith. It suggests picturing to your animal the sun rising and setting for as many days as you will be gone and then picturing yourself happily returning home. The day of our next trip, I sat with Juliette and did this. I told her how many days we would be gone, where we were going, and that my sister would come each day. I told Juliette we would be home before sunset on the third day.

On our return, there she was. We got out of the car. Juliette pranced over to us, rubbed up against Lala, me, and then Evan. She followed us into the house and hung around. That night, she jumped up on the bed and onto my chest. She started to purr, kneading my chest and rubbing her face against mine. She had never done this before. She slept curled up to my side for the first time ever.

Remarkably, Juliette never disappeared again. From that moment forward, I consciously spoke with the animals.

# How to Make Your Vacation Easier on Your Pet

Going on vacation and leaving your animals can be stressful for both you and your pet. Let's make this easier on your animal. Knowledge is power. Tell your animal how long you will be gone. Center yourself, take a couple of deep breaths, and picture the sun rising and setting for as many days as you will be gone. Picture yourself happily returning home. Tell them who will be taking care of them and that you want them to be friends.

Tell them that, if something is wrong, to tell you in the middle of the night because then you will wake up with a feeling that something is wrong.

When you are on vacation, take a moment to quiet yourself and talk with your pet. Send them love; show them, in your mind, things that you have seen or done. The animals will receive these messages and enjoy seeing what you are doing. If you have a hard time creating images in your mind, just make sure your words are clear, and they will receive it.

Having a good caregiver is a must. In my business, I have heard awesome stories of great animal caregivers, but, unfortunately, I have also heard stories that would horrify you. I cannot stress this enough: Do not assume a person or place is going to be good. You have to ask questions and try them out before you leave your animal long-term.

I have a pet-sitter move into my house when I am gone. My animals love her like family. I am incredibly blessed. Some people choose to have a pet-sitter come in for visits; others send them to doggie or kitty daycare/boarding. There are many great options for pet care these days. Please do not send your animal to a traditional kennel or to the veterinarian's office. These are extremely stressful places. There is the noise of the kennels' clank, the lighting is strange, they often hose down the kennels while your dog is in them, and your pet's food and pee schedule will be off. If you choose boarding, choose a place where your animal is going to have fun. Take a tour so you can see exactly where your animal will be kept. Do not just assume a place will be nice. Ask lots of questions!

If you are using a new pet-sitter, have them come over for trial visits. Have them spend time with your pet when you go out for an evening or part of the day. This is a good way for your animal to become comfortable with a new person, to see how your pet is with that particular person, and also a good way to see if the pet-sitter follows your directions and respects your animals and your home. Make sure you ask the pet-sitter just how much time they will be spending with your pet. You may be surprised how short of a time some pet-sitters think is acceptable.

If you have a sick animal, do not settle on the feeling that the pet-sitter is "good enough." There are plenty of people who can administer meds and notice when your animal is not well. If you question whether your pet-sitter will be able to do this and you still like them, hire a veterinary technician to come over and check your animal every day — or at least a few times while you are gone. If you have even a slight reservation or doubt about a pet-sitter, I have learned it's a lot worse than you think it is. Find a new one, right away.

When I talk with animals who have experienced good pet-sitting experiences, they tell me about the places they have walked or the drives they have taken. They talk about how the pet-sitter danced with them or snuggled with them on the couch. They talked about getting snacks or how they wouldn't share their people food. They talk about the music they played or the TV shows they watched. They talk about emergency situations and feeling safe in the care of their sitter. They talk about having fun and being safe, and they offer silly observations.

Some common themes animals talk about when their people are away: they want clean dishes, fresh water, clean litter boxes. Same-time-of day scheduled visits, the same lighting in the house that their owner usually has, open or closed shades/window, play time, pet-sitters not to be on their phones when they are visiting, special snacks, and clothing or bedding that smell like their people.

When I talk to animals who were more stressed, they talk about the lighting in the house being different. Shades closed too much or no lights being on after dark. They talk about not knowing when the pet-sitter is going to show up or the pet-sitter staring at her phone instead of interacting with the pet. They talk about their dishes or litter boxes never getting cleaned. They talk about being scared, lonely, or confused.

Tell the caregiver what your pet likes and dislikes. Have them turn lights on in the house, open shades, and leave the TV or music on. Have them come at the same time each day, so your animal knows what to expect. I always know a good pet-sitter when they say or text things about my pet that makes me know they get my animal's personality. I will never forget the time one pet-sitter left me a note saying that my Australian Shepherd, Stormy, loved to dance with her. This was so true! I loved that she was playing music and dancing with him while I was away.

If you don't hear from them, contact them for updates.

If you feel good with the caregiver, relax and have fun. A good pet-sitter or doggy camp is an adventure for your animals as well.

Take the time to make sure your animal will have a good experience when you are gone. Then enjoy your vacation knowing they are safe and well cared for.

# Fireworks

It is fireworks season again! This is a stressful time of year for even our most confident pets. Random, unpredictable popping and sizzling occur without warning, deafening our animals' ears and confusing their senses. The smell of burning alone can send our animals into "flight" mode.

Remain confident. When I was in college, I didn't understand the concept that animals could be scared of fireworks. My boyfriend and I would take out his sailboat on Long Island Sound to watch the fireworks up close. We would stuff my two dogs' ears full of cotton, and they would sit with us happily all night watching the fireworks. They never once seemed nervous. If we felt safe, they felt safe.

Knowledge is power. Explaining to your animals what is going to happen on the days leading up to the Fourth of July and throughout the weekend can help prepare them for chaos. First, sit in a quiet place with your animals. Remember to breathe and empty your mind of any distractions. While you talk to your animals, picture everything you say as if there are clips of a movie playing in your mind. If you have a hard time visualizing, no worries! Just make sure your words are clear, and your mind will create the pictures on its own. Try to feel every emotion and sense it in your body as if it were happening to yourself at this very moment. Then say to them, "I want to explain to you what will be happening in the next few days (picture a few sunsets and sunrises). Every year on this weekend, adults and children play with toys (picture them with one of their toys and then a human with fireworks). "These human toys make a lot of loud noises (hearing sizzling and popping in your head). They also burn (remember the smell in your mind). They are safe (picture the burning to be exclusively around fireworks). These toys are wonderful for people because they fly high up in the sky and create beautiful, colorful patterns in the sky or on the ground. (Picture the fireworks and people in awe). This happens every year. People all over play with their own fireworks, and then they go to a certain place on one night and watch a big display of fireworks. (Picture people playing joyfully at their home with fireworks and then traveling to where there are crowds and watching a big display).

"I know that it is scary (picture your animal scared), but you are safe, and you must stay home, where you are truly protected. (Picture them confident, aware, and staying home on the Fourth of July). There will be no more fireworks in a few days. (Picture it quiet again after the sun rises and sets a few times). This is what I will do for you on the day when the noise is the worst (explain where they will be and how you will help them.) I love you and want you to feel safe."

This is what you must do: All outside animals should be contained in a safe place. Many animals who would never run away flee in terror on July 4. Please bring them into a safe shelter (garage, laundry room, house). Make sure they cannot climb out of windows or open the doors. At the very least, lock yard gates, but keeping them inside is preferable. Bring all your animals in at least an hour or two before nightfall. Once the noise starts, it will be harder to find them. Close all windows, turn on fans or AC, and leave the TV or light classical music on. Close shades so that the animals do not see the fireworks.

If your animal is frightened inside, you can put a T-shirt on your animal. Safety-pin the shirt around the stomach so it is snug. This can give your dog awareness of its own body and can create more confidence. This concept is much like the "thunder shirt" idea. Some dogs like to go under beds or in a covered crate.

Give your dog a light meal. Eating can affect the limbic system (the emotional center of the brain). If you have to sedate your animal, please tell them what you are doing and the reaction they can expect from the drug so they do not get frightened when they get groggy. If you don't warn them in advance, it can make it worse because they feel disoriented.

We love Young Living essential oils in our house. Diffuse Peace and Calming or rub a little on your dog's back. You can give your animal flower essences. They have a calming effect on animals. You can also try CBD oil or treats to help relax your pets in stressful situations.

I am a Tellington-Touch Practitioner. This work can do wonders for all types of animal situations. Stroking the ears during fearful periods is one method of T-Touch. The T-Touch is a wonderful method to calm and establish a bond with your pet. T-touch is a special way of touching your animal.

Practitioner Jodi Frediani says, "T-Touch likely engages the parasympathetic nervous system, relaxing muscle tension and allowing heart rate, blood pressure, and circulation to slow, in effect bringing stress levels down. Bringing stress levels down may allow a dog (or person or horse) to have more body awareness, which can help if the body is compensating because of a past fear or pain."

Please think of your animal during the Fourth of July Holiday. Take the time to explain to them what will be happening. Be overly cautious about keeping them safe. It can save their lives.

More animals end up lost, dead, or in a shelter on the Fourth of July than on any other day. Some are never found.

Please take the time to take care of your pets — and have an amazing Fourth of July!

# How to "Hear" the Animals

The average pet owner periodically will hear their animal quickly and clearly: "I want to go to beach!" "Give me a spoonful of that ice cream." "My leg hurts." "I love you." "Throw me the ball." "Let me under the covers."

To receive more detailed messages, telepathy is an intense study for anyone who wants to learn.

The first step is self-awareness. If you know yourself well enough, then you will be able to decipher when someone else's thoughts or feelings sneak through your consciousness. Empathic people are constantly sharing information with each other without being aware of it. In fourth grade, I frequently had to leave the classroom because of burning stomachaches. As soon as I would walk down the hallway to the nurse's offices, my stomachaches would disappear. The boy who sat next to me in class had ulcers. I was feeling his pain. This still happens to me today. I'll be on the phone with a client, and my shoulder will start to hurt. I have to ask myself, "Am I hurting because of the way I am sitting, or is this the animal's pain?" I do a check of myself first, and then I ask the animal. Most often, it's the animal's pain.

When we become accustomed to questioning and understanding how we think and feel at any given moment, it is easier to receive our animal's answers when we ask them a question.

How cool! Work on ourselves — hear our animals better! So how do we receive it? First, we have to be able to empty our heads and bodies of thoughts and feelings. Like pouring out a glass and being ready to refill it again. One has to be OK with sitting quietly and letting go of control. It doesn't have to be long. Just a few seconds will do. Once a thought, image, or feeling enters your consciousness, you have to be willing to wait it out, observe it, and, most importantly, not judge it. There, you will find the jewels of how your animal is thinking or feeling. Some people may get flashes of pictures, while others may more easily just have a sense of knowing. No way is better or more efficient than the other. They are all starting grounds for developing more specific telepathy. Sometimes your own thoughts will pop up in the quiet, but, because you are becoming aware of your own process, you recognize it and let it go, willing to start again.

Receiving seems to be the most difficult for people. Ask yourself, "How do I receive information in general?" How do you receive a compliment? How do you receive someone bringing up a serious issue with you? Is it easy to receive love or accept help? How do you handle criticism or bad news about a loved one? The more you are able to remain still within yourself, be patient, wait it out, and feel what is coming toward you, the more the animals will be able to tell you the truth about how they are doing.

Practice talking with your animal, with a question that you know comes with a happy emotion. Fear of the answer can make you run away from staying in the present moment. So, keep it simple and light. What is your favorite thing to do? Your favorite place? Your favorite food? What do you love about me?

Practice feeling the moment when you are at a happy place with your pet, like during a walk or when you're snuggling on the couch. Do you feel the love and the sense of peace that resides in your heart? Can you feel that love and peace connecting you and your animal? Stay with that. Enjoy it. Love it. The more you can open your heart in love and be aware of that moment, the more their incredible thoughts and feelings have a pathway to enter your heart and mind.

Luca, my Poodle, says, "If you try it, you might find that you love yourself more, too."

# Telepathy or Intuition?

I have recently been asked, "What is the difference between telepathy and intuition?" The definition of "telepathy" is: communication from one mind to another by extrasensory means. I would describe forms of "communication" as words forming in the mind, feelings in the body, pictures in the mind, and/or a sense of *knowing*.

"Intuition" is defined as: a quick and ready insight or the ability to understand something immediately, without the need for conscious reasoning.

They are surprisingly similar, and, if they're not studied with intensity, they can often be confused with each other.

In my world, telepathy is consciously communicating with living animals and deceased humans or pets. I do this every day. It is a two-sided conversation. In my mind, using words, feelings, and pictures, I ask an alive animal or deceased being a question. They answer, and vice versa. But sometimes this form of telepathy is one-sided; if someone is thinking strongly, I may pick up bits of their internal dialogue, especially if it has to do with me. One time, I gave a man a present, and I heard him say, "I wonder how much this cost?" I was in shock. *How could someone say that out loud?* But it turns out that he *didn't* say it out loud. He *thought* it.

At times I can hear people talking or thinking about me from a distance. I will be cooking in the kitchen, and, all of a sudden, I will hear their conversation as clearly as if they are on the radio in the background. "You should have a session with Laura." I may hear only bits and pieces of their conversation. The next day, I will get an email from them asking about a session. I often ask myself, "Do I have a really cool super-power?" or "Do I have a kick-ass Spirit Guide on the other side that turns up the volume when I need to be paying attention to a certain personal or business relationship?"

Sometimes this makes people nervous because they think I am going to be reading their thoughts. But I assure you — I don't really care what people are thinking, so I am not listening. I believe in clear verbal communication. If I need to know something, just tell me. If you are judging me in some way, I don't care. You're entitled to your opinion. If this is the case, I am better off concentrating on something else.

Most people who are close to each other have experienced telepathy in their relationships. You're thinking about asking your spouse a question, and then they speak up and answer your question. You reply, "I was just thinking about asking you that," or you think about a friend, and then they call. Or you're out with a friend, and you both decide on going to the same restaurant for lunch. Someone might have thought about it first, and then the other telepathically picked it up and confused it with their own thoughts. You're using telepathy. You are just not conscious of it.

Intuition is different. It's more of an internal knowing or gut feeling that guides you, lets you know what is good or wrong for you, keeps you safe and out of harm's way.

This week, listen to your conversations. Do you recognize any times where you may have sent or picked up a telepathic thought?

# How to Hone Your Intuition

Intuition is defined as: a quick and ready insight or the ability to understand something immediately, without the need for conscious reasoning. "Trust your intuition" is often thrown around when offering advice. But what does this really mean?

My definition of intuition is a gut or heart feeling of what is right and what is wrong. A must-read for everyone is Gavin de Becker's *The Gift of Fear: Survival Signals That Protect Us from Violence*. Gavin de Becker states, "Nature's greatest accomplishment, the human brain, is never more efficient or invested than when its host is at risk. Then, intuition is catapulted to another level entirely, a height at which it can accurately be called graceful, even miraculous. Intuition is the journey from A to Z without stopping at any other letter along the way. It is knowing without knowing why."

Intuition is easy to sense when our decision feels right and it is something that we want. This can be choosing the right pet at the shelter, going on a date with the right person, or taking a great job opportunity. We may not even think too much about it and just react the way we should. One example of this is walking an aggressive dog and suddenly changing up the route. Unbeknownst to us, taking a different route that day helped you to avoid an undesirable encounter with exuberant off-leash dogs. While following our intuition, we feel peaceful and happy. Life seems to flow effortlessly.

Intuition can be harder to listen to when it is screaming at us that something is bad. We don't understand why, and we still want it to be good for us. We meet someone who is charming and respected in the community but still feel a little "off" with them. If we don't listen to this feeling, we may get into an unhealthy business or romantic relationship that betrays us later on. I am the kind of person who wants to believe that all situations and people are innately good. Too many times, I have waited for proof that my intuition is correct and have been traumatized in the process. I have been cheated on by a man I loved and have had a major TV show rip apart my work on national television. I have also felt awkward about my dogs interacting with other dogs — and then see an aggressive incident play out. I am the only one to blame. In these situations, there was something that nagged at me from the beginning that something was off. I chose not to listen because I wanted the situation to be different.

Other times, I have turned down business and romantic proposals that my colleagues and friends would have loved to take themselves. I have decided not to let my dog off leash for no other reason than "it didn't feel right." Each of these times, I found myself blissfully calm and content after stating my decision. Equally so, I have fostered relationships with amazing people that have brought me incredible joy, financial success, and trustworthy friendships. I've found playmates for my dogs that are perfect, and the dogs turn out to be long-lasting best friends.

It is up to each individual to listen to their intuition. If something doesn't feel right, it probably isn't. The more you pay attention to the process of your decisions and the results they manifest, the more confidence you will have in recognizing your intuition. The more you listen to your intuition, the more "in the flow" you will become in life. If you are confused, ask yourself, "What decision will elicit a calm, content feeling inside of me, and what decision feels like stress and turmoil?"

Trust how you feel, act on your decision, and move on, believing that you did what is right for you. Once you have made your decision, don't judge it or change it. Stick with it, and watch the miracles happen.

# Chapter 3

# BEHAVIORAL ISSUES

# Be Open to Possibilities

Jake was three years old when I first met him. He had big, wheat-colored, watchful eyes, silky-black, long-coated fur, and a body like a Golden Retriever. His people signed him up for my six-week intensive dog-training program because he was showing signs of dog aggression. On our first walk, he pulled on the leash, lunging toward a timid Maltese as he foamed at the mouth, growling and barking viciously. To all humans, clearly the Maltese was no threat. It didn't matter what kind of dog was in sight; he acted the same. Although my clients lived on a large estate, they wanted to bring Jake to the beach and to the dog park. They wanted nothing to do with his training. I explained that it's not the best way to set a dog up for success. Dogs need consistency. If they didn't just want Jake to pass other dogs calmly on leash but also run free among a great number of dogs without aggression, they needed to learn about dog training and behavior so that *they* could support him, too. They wanted nothing to do with it. I made no guarantees.

I was too shy to mention my pet-psychic services to Jake's people, but I felt it was important to talk to Jake about what was going on. Jake told me that he had known only dogs that fought for food and/or attention, and that he'd never had a dog friend before.

I asked him where he had lived. He shared that he'd lived in a small dirt yard. Stray dogs would often come and fence-fight or jump into the yard and fight for his bowl of kibble. One day, his people just turned him free. He ended up at a high-kill shelter, where he was taken in by a smaller rescue organization.

I asked Jake how his life has changed. He told me that he feels clean, safe, loved, and cared for. He loves when his people are petting him. He said he feels calm in his yard, listening to the wind, smelling the ocean, watching the squirrels, and playing ball.

I told him that his life with other dogs could be just like that — completely different from his past experiences. I told him that dogs at the beach and the park just want to be calm, happy, and playful, like he feels in his yard. I told him to be open to the possibility of enjoying the company of other dogs and that his future could be better than he could even imagine right now.

He loved this concept. He crawled his big body into my lap and kissed my face.

Remarkably, from that moment on, Jake never barked or lunged at another dog. He ran on the beach and at the park, with a solid "come" when he was called, and a smile on his face. After the six weeks, his people never needed my services again.

Ten years later, I was at the beach when I saw a dog running full speed toward me. When he reached me, he knocked me down, licking my face. It took me a moment. "Oh, my gosh — it's Jake."

He was whining with happiness. "Thank you! Thank you! Thank you for telling me that I can have a life better than I can imagine! I have the best life!" Kneeling, I hugged him; he put his paws on my shoulders, licked my face, and wagged his tail. Tears streamed from my eyes. "I am so proud of you, Jake."

I was amazed that he remembered me, smelled me from so far away, and that what I'd said had had such a big impact on him, even 10 years later.

I think of him many times each month when I tell other rescue animals about Jake and how he changed. "You know others like me?" they respond. "They changed?"

Because of him, other animals live happier lives. During hard times, I remember Jake's courage, too. I contemplate how his people's detachment from Jake's aggressive behavior and their confidence that he could change may have played an integral part in his evolution.

# Teaching Your Pets
# Impulse Control

We all have an idea of what impulse control is. It is what stops us from having that second piece of cake or glass of wine, holds us back from blurting out an inappropriate comment, stops us from cheating on our spouses, and is what propels us into doing what is morally right when a part of us wants to do the "wrong thing." The more conscious we are of our thoughts and actions, the more impulse control we have.

Hudson, my sweet, intelligent, goofy, 100-pound, 3.5-year-old male German Shepherd went after another dog a few weeks back, thinking that he was protecting Felix, my Chihuahua, from being harmed. Hudson has a soft mouth, so he didn't hurt the other dog, but because of his size and his breed, it was scary and inappropriate. Some are quick to judge him a "bad dog" and claim that I should "put him to sleep," while others are equally quick to dismiss it because "dogs will be dogs," and he was "protecting his little brother" and, besides, he is a powerful German Shepherd who "chose" not to hurt the other dog.

I saw it as me failing him. Somewhere, there was a break in our training, and it's my job to figure out where that is and to correct it, so Hudson can make better decisions in the future. I immediately understood where in the incident I could have done better. Three minutes before the incident, Hudson came to me overwhelmed. He knew the Border Collies we were with, but they were un-neutered and doing their herding behaviors with a ball and with each other. Hudson didn't understand their crouching-down, seemingly erratic behaviors and came to me for help. I thought about leashing him then and putting him in a "Down. Stay," but, for some reason, I didn't. I believe I was telling myself he needed more exercise because he had been in the house all day. When he felt Felix was in danger, he reacted instead of thinking it through, and that was clearly my fault. How could he think it through when he was already expressing confusion?

Dogs thrive when they have impulse control. They are calmer and more thoughtful. I had to ask myself, "Where is impulse control lacking in his life?" I knew immediately. Hudson, like many other dogs, has a strong prey drive. Since he was young, we have spent many hours a day on ranches where Hudson was allowed to — and, in some cases, praised for chasing gophers away from the fields. I told myself it was good exercise for him. He was safe. He didn't catch them. He just chased them.

After the incident, Hudson went into my boot camp. He was going to learn impulse control. On walks, he is either on a 6-foot or 16-foot leash, and he won't graduate from that for a while. I was amazed at what I noticed at first. The sound of a gopher or the sight of something moving fast put Hudson into immediate stress. He would quickly stand erect and almost shiver with the energy of wanting to chase. Gently, he would pull a bit at the end of the leash. Not with all his power, but definitely testing me. Sometimes he would come to me and body-block me with his sides and hips. The average person might think it was playing, but he was testing his dominance on me. How had I missed this? "Hudson is stressed!" I quickly noticed. What I thought was a fun pastime for Hudson was actually causing him distress. I was sad for him, and it was my duty to find ways to fix it.

It is not uncommon to see an increase in aggression and/ or dominance in the three- to four-year-old range. I had to take all of this seriously. I upped his training immediately. Gently getting his attention back on me with "Leave its," "sits," "downs," "waits," "stays, "heels," and playing with me instead of feeling like he had to be hyper-vigilant about his surroundings. It took a few weeks, but the results have been remarkable. He is calmer all around. He can watch a bunny or a gopher run across the trail five feet in front of him without stiffening and feeling like he has to chase. He is body-blocking me and his siblings less or rarely at all. He watches out the window with more awareness and a calmer demeanor. He is still my goofy, playful Hudson, but he is surprisingly more confident and secure. I can see it in his eyes. I have shown up for him, and, because of it, he is thriving. Impulse control, boundaries, and training are not just fun exercises now. They are for his well-being and will continue to be part of our daily way of life forever. Little things go a long way. "Waits" in and out of the door. "Down stays" in environments where they need to watch instead of being involved. "Look at me" when they become focused on something else. Less freedom off leash instead of more.

I had clients the other day who have a nervous cocker spaniel. They live in the country. This dog will see people, bunnies, squirrels, or cats outside the window and then run out the dog door, barking, run around the yard, and then come back into the house, finally settling down. The dog is allowed to do this because no neighbors complain and because the dog is "getting exercise." But this is no different than what I was allowing with Hudson. This dog's adrenal and stress hormones are pumping through her. These stressful behaviors are not helping her self-confidence in other areas of her life. These periods of stress are teaching her that, when she is confused, it's OK and even normal to get riled up. It will be interesting to see if these people close the dog door and implement the same type of training I did with Hudson.

I urge you to look at your stressed, naughty, dominant, or fearful dog and ask yourself, "Where am I allowing him/her to have no impulse control, resulting in higher stress hormones?" and then ask yourself, "What can I do to help my dog calm down, so he/she can make better decisions?"

Sometimes the hardest part of fixing a problem is first looking inward. I have found that the more conscious of my behavior I get, the happier and calmer in life I am. Change first starts with the person. Then with the pet. There is no fault in admitting one can do better. So, take the time to think, and ask, "What have I been doing wrong?"

Then praise yourself, and enjoy it when you get it right. The rewards are great.

# Calling All Off-Leash Dog Owners

"Can you put your dog on leash?" "Please call your dog away from us." "This dog has issues." "This dog is frightened." "My dog might kill your dog." These are all things I have screamed to people when walking a troubled dog on leash.

"My dog is friendly!" I often hear back with no action taken to leash their dog or to call their dog to them.

"This dog is not!" I will scream. If you ever hear this, take it seriously.

If I am farther away, I might hold up the end of the leash and shake it so that the dog owner in the distance can see that my dog is on leash. I might put my dog in heel and move off to the side. I might put the dog in sit or a down-stay or hold out a treat to get them focused on me. I might reach into my bag and start putting my dog into a gentle leader or a muzzle.

People and dogs who are acting in the way that I just explained need your help. They need you to be present for a moment. Please think about this.

As off-leash dog owners, you have the responsibility to be watching your surroundings for this situation. If someone asks you to leash your dog, do not take it personally against you or your dog. Do not feel your dog can handle that dog. Don't get mad, annoyed, or frustrated. I am going to be very harsh here. Don't be stupid and let your dog approach this situation.

As a conscious pet owner, you have to realize that not all dogs are as well socialized as yours and that these dogs and their people need your help. They need you to be watching out for them and helping them have a good experience. It may be an inconvenience for you, but they need you to show them that your dog will not approach them. How do you do this?

If you have an exuberant dog that may run over to them or try to get close, leash your dog until they have passed you and you are confident your dog will not run after them. These troubled dogs may not be able to read that your dog is not a threat.

If you have a dog that you can control with voice commands or that you are confident will stay away, show the person that your dog is cool. Call your dog to you. Reach down and pet your dog. Wave to that person. Just do something that says, "I hear you. My dog is under control."

If you have a dog that is ball obsessed and you know your dog couldn't care less about the other dog, wave to the other dog owner and show them something that says, "He/she is all about the ball. Don't worry." Then watch to see how that dog reacts when you throw the ball. If it looks stressed and excitable, hold the ball and keep your dog still until they pass.

If you continue throwing the ball, make sure you do it in the opposite direction.

If you are walking in the direction of someone who has just asked you to leash your dog or showed you in some way that they are troubled, watch them. Are they trying to get organized? Are they ready for you to pass them? You may need to slow down or stop for a moment. Maybe you need to walk quickly past them. Or it may be best that you stand still and they pass you, or perhaps it is OK for you both to keep walking and pass each other.

I know that this can sound like a lot of work, but it isn't.

You and your dog's behavior in these moments can have an enormous impact on the emotional well-being of these troubled dogs and their handlers. Little successes will build confidence in these dogs and their handlers. If you allow your dog to approach, these dogs might become aggressive to the point that they may knock down their people, lunge at your dog, bite your dog, and seriously harm your dog.

You may say that these dogs should not be out with their people, but in fact, these dogs may be more well-trained than your own. They may know advanced obedience commands, tricks, do canine sports, and be therapy dogs. If not, they may be in a training program to help them through their fear, aggression, and anxiety. These are intelligent dogs that either have been through trauma or have the genetics that cannot handle being in an environment with fast movements or being approached by another dog. They may have been attacked by other dogs at some time in their life or abused by people. They may have high-stress hormones passed down from their mothers, or they may have been strays that have learned that an approaching dog usually means a fight for territory. Their handlers are doing their very best to get their dogs out for joy, exercise, training, and socialization. These dogs need to be set up for success.

I want you to understand that these dogs may look very happy and well socialized from a distance, but once your dog crosses that comfort zone, these dogs may go into flight-or-fight response, which is very similar to a human who has post-traumatic stress. When these animals are pushed past their comfort zones, instincts for survival kick in; it may be hard for their handlers to control them, and a disaster may occur. Their comfort zones may be thirty feet, twenty feet, or five feet. A perceived bad experience can set these dogs back months.

If these dogs and people have a good experience when they are out, they are closer to overcoming their fear and aggression. These dogs may one day be able to greet dogs in a controlled environment or even run free.

If you love dogs, take all of this to heart.

The people who are handling these dogs are doing the very best they can. They may have never known an aggressive or fearful dog before, and they are doing their very best to get their dogs socialized and give them a joyful life. Some of these people have been through trauma themselves trying to contain their dogs from going after or running away from other dogs that have approached them. Some of these people have fallen, been bitten trying to break up a fight, or just empathically traumatized by seeing their dog struggle.

So, if a handler is frantically yelling at you to leash your dog, don't take it personally. They are just being triggered into a post-traumatic stress response by your unleashed dog. Just take a breath, and do one of those things I mentioned to let them know, "All will be fine. I have my dog under control."

When you leave the home to walk your dog, there is no worry. It is just going out to play and exercise the dog. But when these handlers leave their home, they are working very hard on creating an enjoyable, positive experience for their dog. They are replacing thoughts of "I hope we don't have an incident." with "This walk is going to be awesome. We can handle this."

So, when you are out with your dog, keep an eye out for these situations. If you see a dog on leash in the distance or even under the table at a restaurant, ask yourself, "How is their person responding by seeing you and your dog? Are they getting out treats or putting different equipment on their dog? Are they asking their dog to heel or pay attention to them?"

If so, help them out without being asked. You will make their day! They probably will pass you with gleaming smiles, extreme gratitude, and tons of praise to their dog. That night they will be bragging to their friends and family how well their dog did and how they had such an awesome walk. It's true. I have been that person

Spread the word on this. These dogs and people are everywhere you walk. They need our compassion and our help.

Thank you.

# Litter Box Issues

There is not a week that goes by that someone does not call me with, "Help! My cat is peeing and pooping outside the litter box!" These cats do their excretions on piles of clothing, the kitchen counter, stovetops, the toaster, the bathroom sink, walls, in shoes, on paintings, and even on computer keyboards.

This can be going on for days or for years. After a few adjustments on the human's part and/or communication, this undesirable behavior often stops.

I have heard it all. Here are some quotes from cats about this behavior:

> *"I pee on the stove because it's cool on my feet. My pee stings really bad."*

> *"I pee and poop on the floor outside the litter box because I have such bad constipation it hurts to step into the litter box … I know I still jump on the couch. But when I have to go, it hurts worse."*

> *"I can't control it."*

> *"Sometimes, the poop gets stuck in me, and then it just comes out."*

"I can't make it to the litter box. I am leaking all day."

"Have you ever been in that litter box? It stinks really bad. I am not going in there until they take off the top."

"The litter burns my paws."

"The litter is so dusty it hurts my eyes and my breathing."

"I want my person to watch TV with me more (Dancing with the Stars, to be exact)."

"I just want my person to say 'Hello' to me when they come home."

"I am worried about my person's health. They need to go to the doctor, and he is not listening to me."

"I hate my person's new spouse. That is why I pee in her shoes. Please tell him to get rid of her."

"I am guarding the house from the invasion of other cats in the neighborhood. My smell needs to be here."

"My mind is not working right. I am getting disoriented and confused. The smell helps me get around the house."

"We have too many visitors. I don't like what goes on in all of their minds."

"I am marking my territory. I am being bullied by the other cats in the house."

"Smelling my urine helps me feel more comfortable when my person is away."

*"I am confused. My people are talking about moving. Am I going with them?"*

*"I am stressed. My people are fighting and are unhappy. It makes me unhappy."*

*"I feel it's a good thing. I know you are like, 'Gross. It's not a good thing. You are ruining the home.' But I feel like our kids like me doing it because they are like, 'Kitty is showing our mom something about ourselves.' I feel like they are like, 'Phew. Kitty is showing mom how we feel.' They don't want to go to their dad's anymore."*

*"The litter box makes noise after I leave it. I think it's going to come after me."*

*"Have you ever seen how dirty the litter box is? They rarely clean it."*

*"My brother's (cat) pee smells so bad. I can't stand to go in there after him."*

*"The new furniture smells. I needed to make it smell like home."*

*"Because I have been declawed, my paws cramp, and I hate the way the litter feels on my skin."*

Because of this problem, I have seen humans dump cats in a strange neighborhood, put them to sleep, find them a new home, make them an outdoor-only cat, or send them to a rescue organization.

My Snowshoe cat, Ella, was returned to the shelter three times and picked up as a stray once before I adopted her. The shelter staff told me, "You don't want that cat! She pees outside the litter box. Everyone returns her." I went into the cat room and sat with Ella. I told her all about the six other animals at home and what her life would look like if I adopted her. She told me she peed outside the litter box because she doesn't see well, and the people were very messy; they also walked very fast, almost running into her. She said everyone was so angry with her that she felt insecure and not loved. Peeing made her feel more confident. I told her she will always be loved at my house. I couldn't guarantee that my young German Shepherd wouldn't run into her, and that she must only pee outside or in the litter-box. I told her I would give her the night to think about it and would be back the next day. The next day, she told me she wanted to come home with me. Ella pees and poops in two places: in her litter box and in some gravel by the outdoor garbage cans. She has been perfect for the years she has been with me.

Here are the top quick fixes for this problem. Please give your cat a few weeks to change their behavior. Sometimes the behavior gets worse before it gets better, but keep firm in your mind what you want of your cat and how much you love them.

1.  Take your cat to the vet to rule out urinary tract infection, crystals, diabetes, IBD, tumors, and kidney problems. These cats pee where they sleep, on cold surfaces like tile or in the tub, rugs, and on clothing.

2. Feed them high-quality cat food, so they do not get these medical problems. Make sure your brand of cat food is not owned by a candy company — for obvious reasons.

3. Take the top off the litter box. Tops lock in the strong scent of cat pee and make your cat nauseous. Have the litter box in a well-ventilated, low-traffic location.

4. Use a dust-free litter. Many cats have a hard time breathing in the dust that is created by clay litter. Make sure your litter doesn't have those colored pellets. The cats talk about them burning their paws.

5. Clean the litter box often. Cats are neat freaks and hate to walk on their own poop and pee.

6. Put out multiple boxes. Have a litter box for each cat. Many don't like to share, or they use one for urine and one for poop. If you have a large house or two stories, put boxes in several locations, especially for the very young and the very old.

7. Experiment with the depth of the litter. Older cats with hip and knee problems like to have less litter so that their joints don't have to work as hard when they squat. Sometimes using a pee pad is better.

8.  Experiment with the size of the litter box. Some older cats have a hard time stepping into a litter box where the sides are tall. Creating a ramp or another step into the box helps.

9.  Make sure the litter box is not touching a wall. Some cats like to stand on the side, so they need space around the box.

10. Have at least a fifteen minute period during the day, at the same time every day, that you give your cat your undivided attention. (Pet, brush, play, talk to, give treats, look at, listen to).

11. If your cat is peeing only when a certain person is coming over, get rid of that person. From my experience concerning this issue, cats are usually ninety-eight percent of the time a good judge of character.

12. Talk to your animals about their relationships with the other animals in the house. Praise bonding time and loving behaviors.

13. Most important: Explain to your cat, "When you pee and poop outside the litter box it makes me upset. Please pee and poop in the litter box. I am trying to figure out what is wrong. Can you give me another sign to show me what is wrong?"

14. Then watch your cat closely. Watch how they walk. Are they sore around their hip area (kidneys)? Do they strain to pee? Are they getting bullied? Are they hiding in dark places? If you just take the time to watch with no judgments, the solution may be obvious. Often cats use peeing and pooping behavior to communicate that they want to tell you something.

15. Marking is an instinctual behavior to help animals feel safe. Is there something going on at home or outside that would make them feel vulnerable? What can you do and say to your animal to help them feel better?

16. Watch your own emotional state. Are you feeling safe in all aspects of your life? Do you get along with others? Do you communicate your emotions in a healthy way? Are you pissed off? Get off your phone, and spend time meditating, relaxing, and being present. Often our animals' behavior is a reflection of the emotional state of the home. Be at peace, be grateful, have fun, and enjoy their company.

# Behavioral Issues Can Be Due to Pain in the Body

Often people and veterinarians will contact me to find out what is physically wrong with an animal. A horse may have some strange behavioral problems, or an animal might be limping or panting, and no one can figure out the cause of the issue. An animal may have a diagnosis and be in treatment, but they are still not thriving. I cannot diagnose an illness, but I can find out exactly how an animal is feeling, what the pain's intensity level is, and if the animal knows what makes the pain better or worse. I can relate that to other animals and what their diagnoses were. Oftentimes, this information will help veterinarians know where to look in the body and how to better treat the animal's symptoms.

Dane was a shepherd mix. He was a seizure-alert dog that suddenly stopped alerting his person to her seizures. No one, not even the veterinarian, could figure out why. When Dane spoke with me, he told me that he had a deep pain in his left ear. It caused him so much pain that he had a hard time concentrating. The veterinarian looked in his ear and found an infected eardrum. Once that was treated, he started to seizure-alert again.

A cat named Lilly told me she was biting her people because she had a sharp pain in her neck and head. Whenever her people went to pet her, she would lift her head up higher. This caused a pinch in a nerve to the point where she was overwhelmed with a sharp tingling sensation up and over her head (similar to an ice-cream headache or diving into freezing-cold water). She would then react out of intense pain and fear and bite her people. Lilly was adjusted by a chiropractor and put on a natural anti-inflammatory herb. As soon as the pain was gone, she stopped biting.

Pablo is a Quarter Horse. He started to refuse jumps and buck his rider off. The trainers swore it was behavioral, but his person felt differently. Pablo told me that his new saddle hurt his back. It pinched him badly at his withers and came down hard on his back when his rider would sit deep. His owner got him a better-fitting saddle, and he never refused a jump or bucked his rider off again.

Mable the cat was acting lethargic. She told me that, when she breathed in, it felt like cold, shallow air in her chest. In my experience, this could be a heart problem, something going on with the lungs, or the need for a chiropractic adjustment. I urged her people to take her to the vet. During an ultrasound, sadly, they found lung cancer.

So, do you need to be a pet psychic to figure out what your animal is feeling? No, I don't believe you do. But I do believe you have to be aware, and you have to be in tune with your own body. Oftentimes, the animals will tell you how they feel. They will send you their own feelings, trying to get you to experience these feelings in your own body. People may pick up these messages as feelings in their own body but misinterpret them as their own. I do this all the time. Whenever I feel pain or discomfort when I am around a person or animal, I have to consciously ask myself or the animal, "Is this my pain or theirs? How are they feeling?"

For instance, a dog may have a hurt shoulder, and his human may intermittently start complaining about shoulder pain. A cat may have an infected tooth, and the person may find themselves rubbing their hand on their own jawline. If the issue is not addressed, it can get much more serious — to the point that we take on each other's pains and illness. A cat has kidney problems, and the human may have a kidney infection. Or it can go the other way — a human has a broken heart, and the animal is diagnosed with heart problems.

If you suspect your animal has an issue, ask them to over-exaggerate where they hurt or how they are feeling so that you can see with your own eyes what is going on. Tell them that you want to know and to please show you with their behavior.

You can also tell them to send you the feelings they have in their bodies. Tell them to concentrate on being clear and to send you exactly how they feel. It may not be right at that moment that you feel it, but, throughout the day, check in with yourself, and see how your body is feeling. There is a high probability that you will feel your animal's issues. If you do feel something different, ask yourself, "How long have I been feeling that? Did I injure myself? Eat something? Is this mine? Or is this my animal's?" After some practice with this, you will be able to quickly decipher these feelings and know if they belong to you, your pet, or a person around you.

If you suspect that your animal is being empathic to your emotional or physical feelings, tell them it is OK to let your negative feelings go and to concentrate on joy and the pleasure of living a happy, healthy life. Spend time focusing on what makes you happy and healthy. Spend time being grateful. Spend time creating how you want to feel and enjoy the present moment. It is wonderful to be conscious of how you and your animals are feeling. Then, once you know, work and live in a place of creating joy and health. Believe in the modalities you are using to change those feelings. Believe that life and health *can* get better, no matter what.

# Scaredy Horse?
# How to Ease
# an Animal's Fears

Awoman called me about her 11-month-old Oldenburg stallion named Shiva. She, the trainers, and the farrier were having a hard time getting him to lift his back legs — a necessity for all horses. They thought he would grow out of it, but he wasn't. Shiva was getting big, and his behavior was getting dangerous. He was kicking at them hard.

He made me laugh when he asked me quite quickly, "There is a big horsefly that is bothering me right now. Can you please get rid of it?" Then he said, "I want you to tell my mom that I want to go to the class where you walk me into a room (the arena), and everyone says how pretty and handsome I am. When do we do that? I am so excited for that." Shiva had an amazing pedigree. He was bred to be shown. If his behavior changes, he would be showing off his beauty soon.

Then it was time to talk about his feet. I explained to him why people need to lift up his back hooves, to clean and trim them, and then I asked him why he was being so violent. He answered, "When they are trying to pick up my hooves, I feel like they are trying to push me off balance to knock me over. Are they going to tie my legs? It feels like they are."

He sent me a very clear image of him being knocked over (similar to alpha-rolling a dog) and someone rubbing his belly. People do not typically do this to horses. It was alarming.

I assured him that he would always remain standing, that he could easily balance himself, and that his back legs would never be tied. He skewed up his courage and offered, "Do you think that maybe they could stroke my legs, like they do with my front legs?"

I told him, "Of course."

But he could not let it go and continued, "I really feel like I am going to fall over. You know what else they did? They burned me really bad."

It took us humans a few moments. Then we figured it out. When Shiva was much younger, they hobbled him, tying his back legs, and then branded him, which resulted in him freaking out and falling over. They probably rubbed his belly to soothe him in the chaos.

I was worried that this experience had been imprinted in him, but I also believe wholeheartedly that animals can raise their consciousness above instinct. I explained to him what had happened to him, promised him it would never happen again, and told him that, if he wanted to be champion, he had to lift up his hooves kindly and stop all of his dangerous kicking.

He replied, "I feel like I understand you now. I want to be the best horse I can be. I want to be special for my mom. What else can I do? Can we jump? Can I play with the toy ball and move it around the paddock? Tell my mom I love it when she grabs my crest mane and brings me to her. Can she scratch the side of my face more?"

From that moment on, Shiva lifted up his back hooves gracefully and never kicked out at another person again. I am so proud of him for overcoming his fear.

Some beings will gain understanding and let go of an inappropriate behavior instantly. Shouldn't we hold this space and potential for them, rather than so easily labeling animals "mean," "stubborn," or "dangerous" when, inside, they are just confused and scared?

You don't have to be a pet psychic to take the time to explain to an animal that they are safe and why you need them to act a certain way. Doing so raises their consciousness, fosters courage, and gives them a reason to try to do their best for you.

# Feel Discomfort in Your Home? Be Aware

In September of 2018, I noticed that Felix, my seven-year-old Chihuahua mix, started to look forlorn. It took him a few extra moments to launch off the couch for a walk. When I brought out treats, he would comply with sit, shake, twirl, beg, but his eyes were not as big as normal when offering his trick repertoire. Then I noticed he periodically started to lift his leg on the table by the front door. Of course, I never caught him in this act, but I knew it was him. At the time of his adoption five years ago, he went through a period like this.

Now, granted, Felix did not always look upset. He still ran through his agility course with a big smile, did his zoomies on walks, and played with Luca, my Poodle. Though, coincidently, during this period, he started to become a little more distant with my housekeeper.

One does not win Felix's trust easily. It takes a lot of patience with the "I trust you/I don't trust you" dance until you are in Felix's inner circle. When you are in his circle, you can pet him, snap on his leash, and, best of all, have him snuggle in your lap like a baby. My housekeeper was once in his inner circle, but now, he was more standoffish with her and looked at her with an untrusting eye.

I asked Felix many times what was wrong. He never had a satisfying answer. "I don't know," he would say. "I just feel 'off.' It's not pains in my body. I just felt like peeing. I don't want to go to her right now. I don't want her to touch me." It was frustrating and worrisome for me. I had him adjusted by a chiropractor, upped his CBD oil, and made sure I gave him extra attention each day.

In November 2018, my purse was stolen out of the house while I was on a walk with my dogs, and then I started noticing little things missing or misplaced. I noticed that precious jewelry that had been in my family for generations had been stolen out of my key safe. Only three people knew of that safe. Long story short, it turned out that my housekeeper and an estranged friend had teamed up to steal. The day I fired my housekeeper, my front gate mysteriously locked shut. Even the locksmith couldn't open it. I took it as a sign from Spirit that my home was now secure.

The next day, Felix was completely back to normal. It's been a month now, and he has not peed once in the house. He offers his trick repertoire without being prompted and launches himself off the couch at the slightest hint that we are going on a walk.

The odd thing is that *I* felt like Felix, too. After I fired her and had the locks changed, I felt strangely happier. I did go through a period of shock, knowing that people I'd trusted for so long had betrayed me, but I also felt relief from stress that I didn't even know I had. I found that interesting.

I asked Felix if he knew she was stealing, and he answered, "I didn't know she was stealing, but I felt a pressure of discomfort in the house. Seeing her, I felt uneasy in my stomach. When you fired her, I felt as if the air was cleaner. I just felt happier. I learned that the way you feel in general can have something to do with the character of people around you. People should be more discerning about who they care deeply about. I have done a lot of work on learning how to be brave around people. If I feel 'off' around someone now, there is probably a reason.

"Trust only people and animals that want to become wiser about themselves. Trust your feelings, and surround yourself with people whose stories you don't ever feel like you have to question. Don't hate others or react badly to others. Just peacefully love the ones who deserve to be loved. That is what I am going to do." My little Felix has come a long way. I tell him all the time that he has changed his personality. He gets bright-eyed and smiley at that, because he knows it's true.

# A Conversation on Eating Strange Things

Dhatri was adopted from the DAWG Rescue Organization. He is of small, stocky stature. He is a handsome, cream-colored Dachshund mix with ears that can stand up like a German Shepherd's or flop over while he is sleeping. He was twelve-years-old at the time of this session in May 2017. His person (mom) had contacted me to see how he was feeling and to tell him to stop eating strange things on their walks. He recently had to spend some time in the hospital because he'd eaten dirt and pebbles. He has also been known to eat cactus.

People often ask me if animals speak to one another. The answer is "Yes" — they do it all the time. Here is Dharti's story:

Dhatri shares, "When I was in the hospital, there was this woman there who said I couldn't be cuter and that I reminded her of an old dog she had that died. I felt special at that moment. It was like she loved me, but she loved her other dog *through* me. I was a beacon of memory for her. It was a special feeling. I wondered if, after I die, my mom would meet a dog like me."

Because Dhatri was very sick, I asked if he felt he was going to die soon.

He replied, "I sure did think so, but I don't feel like I am dying now. In the hospital, a cat died. I saw her spirit get up and do this crazy cat stretch, meow, and then she leaped through the Universe. I was like, 'Wow! Cats go to Heaven, too!' Dhatri doesn't like cats.

"I eat stuff because I am curious if it might soothe my stomach. I don't have a burning stomach; I just have a lining in my stomach that feels good with food in it. I eat because it soothes me, like the feeling of snuggling in a comforter." It's possible that he is seeking minerals and probiotics by eating dirt and pebbles. But not cacti!

I told him the veterinarian said he might have to wear a muzzle when he goes for walks.

He replied, "Laura, I am not an attacker."

Then Dahtri shared with me a conversation he had with a dog he met: "One time, I saw a Husky dog with a gentle leader, and I was like, 'Why do you have a teeth restrictor on?'"

"The Husky said, 'It's not restricting my teeth. It's trying to get me to slow down.'

"I (Dhatri) said, 'Just slow down, then.'

"The Husky said his people walk too slowly and that this device made them feel more in control about how fast they moved together.

"I said to the dog, 'That looks uncomfortable.'

"The Husky said, 'You get used to it. I'd rather have this than the choking collar.'

"Then I said, 'What's 'the choking collar'?'

"He said, 'It is just what it sounds like.'

"Then I thought to myself, *Humans are so weird to dogs. I mean, it's weird how humans think. Put a muzzle on me? That is like them going in the shower with their hands tied.*"

Dhatri then waited for my response. I asked him, "How so?"

Dhatri replied, "Of course, I need my mouth to go for a walk! How else to lick, communicate with other dogs, and open my mouth to breathe? That is a stupid question, Laura."

Then he shared, "I feel like my soul has been around for many lifetimes. I will be around in this life for many years. When I die, I will reincarnate back to my mom. I feel like my mom and I need to be together forever."

I always need to get back to the point, so I reiterated, "You'd better stop eating strange things, so you can get the most out of this life."

# Why Is the Show Horse, Easy, Suddenly Having a Difficult Time?

Easy is a seven-year-old Oldenburg horse. He is a big bay with a white blaze and big, soulful eyes. Although he is young, he has won many championships. He just recovered from an injury and is back to showing again. Easy's trainer booked an appointment because, at their last show, Easy's whole demeanor had changed. He was spooky at the jumps even though he'd been ridden and lunged pretty hard before his classes. Easy may dip his shoulder after a jump, trying to throw his rider. His trainer feared that this behavior might carry forward and that his owner would want to sell him.

This is a common reason that equine professionals reach out to me. Horses suddenly become spooky and dangerous in the show ring or around the show grounds, and I am a last resort for figuring out what has changed and how these horses can be helped. Often, it's pain. These are high-level athletes who need chiropractic adjustments, massages, better saddle fittings, and supplements. If the trainers and riders are cutting-edge, then these horses are already getting these treatments regularly in their schedule. Other reasons for changes in behavior are abuse from riders and/or handlers or some type of post-traumatic stress response.

I could tell by Easy's trainer's questions on my intake form that Easy was trained and cared for in a consciously kind way. He wrote, "Are you OK?" "Is there something I can do to help?" "How can I make you happier?" I am used to receiving angrier questions, like, "What the hell is wrong with you?" "Stop doing ..." and "Do you know this is your job?"

Just because a horse has pain in his body doesn't mean that he will act spooky or dangerous. Sometimes they are more lethargic, depressed, or tender when you put their tack on. When an animal is spooky, they are not able to think clearly. Their state of mind is fear. It is my job to get these horses to understand how to self-soothe with a rider on top of them, how and why it's important to pay attention to the rider when they are in a state of stress, and the consequences of throwing and/or injuring a rider.

I was in awe about how much Easy loves his trainer, John. He said, "I love it when John rides me. I get in the groove. I feel good in my body, and I can stretch out, but, other times, I get this poking sensation on the right side of my jaw. Then I get a massive cramp in my hind end. When that happens, I get angry and all worked up.

"John is really clear in his head with me. I always know what is coming next. I'm so grateful for that."

When I asked Easy why he was so spooky at that last show and why his demeanor is changing, he said, "Because my horse friend died there. I might get sick. I don't want to get anything contagious."

John gasped and said, "Wait — what?" He took a moment to think and then shared that, exactly a year ago, one of their horses got sick and died at that very same show.

Easy remembers. He remembers the fear of not knowing what made the horse sick. He remembers the suffering of his friend and his friend dying. He had been carrying that confusion for a whole year. I explained to him that he has vaccinations, that he is not going to get sick at shows, that his friend is in Heaven, and that it is safe to go to that venue.

Ever since our talk, Easy is much calmer.

These animals are deeply conscious beings. Just like people, they mourn, need situations explained to them, and want to know what is happening next. Open your heart and mind, talk with them, and trust that they will understand.

# *Behavioral Problem?*
# *Aren't I Perfect?*

My last session of the day was a five and a half pound male Yorkie named Tao and his person, Kazumi. They live in Tokyo, Japan. When I opened up their file, I knew the session was going to be interesting. Kazumi had sent me five pictures of Tao where he was staring directly into the camera with a serious-looking face. Kazumi wrote on their intake form, "Tao is extremely smart and cautious. A dog expert said he is easily frightened and shy, which is probably true. It's hard for him to cope with any new situation. He is always on edge, barking. He is a vigilante. Is there anything my husband and I can do to make his life more enjoyable and help him to be less reactive?"

I was expecting to hear a timid dog, but that is not what happened. Tao opened with, "My mom talks to me all the time, but I get confused. She tells me to be a good boy, but I feel I am already perfect. I have a hard time finding 'more perfect' because I am already perfect."

I mentioned that his mom was talking about his reactivity and asked him if he could explain how he feels when he barks. Tao answered, "I feel like my heart and mind have a separation. My heart jumps away from peace, while my mind collapses and searches. I am confused because I don't have a sniff on where to go. I forget everything I know. I fall into a strange dog. It's not me — it's another me. What helps me the most is that ring toy with the really good meat smell on it." There is a lot of information in this statement. When Tao gets overwhelmed, he gets distracted and stressed. Kazumi mentioned that they sometimes do scent-training, and she knows the toy he is talking about. It is clear that having a scent object on walks will help Tao regain his focus when he is overwhelmed.

He then shared, "I find my life with my mom totally enjoyable. She would love to clone me. I am so perfect. Dad thinks I am perfect, too. Sometimes he gets frustrated with me. I tell him, 'Dad, I never get frustrated with you. I know you're a hard worker. You just need a nap.' I tell my dad that all the time. If I get really busy with my mom, I get sleepy and cranky, too. When dad naps, he is like a dead bird." Tao's family is definitely getting across how much they love him! He seems like a confident guy to me.

"I am not very reactive," he said. "I get annoyed when neighbors make noise. I hate the sound of the heater for the clothes. Outside, barking is my way of saying, 'I am a great presence in this world. Do you see my great presence?' I am little, so I have to be loud to feel big."

I explain to him that his energy is scattered and that he needs to walk with a calm, quiet confidence and trust his people more to take care of the situation. I show him with pictures what that looks like and the different feelings it produces. I show him the difference between what he does and what we would like him to do.

He thought for a moment and said, "Don't be my reactive self, saying, 'I'm here.' Instead, be a part of the calm world … like an animal that is watching you that you don't notice until you look at it. That is an interesting thought because I have never done that before."

I told him to become one with everything and to trust the presence of his mom. He said, "I am one with everything when I am doing sniff dog training."

I am reminded once again that, just because a dog is five and a half pounds, they need more than just being told they are perfect. Just like a German Shepherd, they also need training to feel calm in the world. I commend Kazumi for introducing Tao to scent training. What else can this smart little guy get excited about learning?

# "The Gangster" vs. "The Peaceful Pup": Labels We Give Our Pets

So often we put labels on animals. Some of them sound like this: "She is aggressive." "He is shy and was abused." "He will run you over." "She is neurotic and barks at everything." "He runs off." "She has separation anxiety." "She's mad when we go away and pees on the carpet." "He hates skateboards."

When we put these labels on our animals, they become stuck in the behavior. Now, don't get me wrong. It's important to notice an undesirable behavior and take steps to change it. But it is also important to watch what you are saying and thinking while you are doing that. I can't tell you how many times I have noticed people working hard on changing a behavior with training but still labeling their animals with the behavior they don't want. I have been guilty of this myself. It takes real awareness to see it.

In 2014, I adopted a Chihuahua mix from the Downey Shelter. This is a hardcore kill shelter. Felix was scheduled to be euthanized the day he was rescued. He had been a stray for some time and was un-neutered as well. When he first came here, he was food aggressive, would snap at people when they tried to pet him, and would lunge, chase, and bite fur off dogs that approached him or ran in his vicinity. I labeled him "The Gangster." This labeled suited him to the point that, after witnessing his behavior, it got many chuckles. But what was I doing, really?

In the year after I rescued Felix, he was making great progress. He set appropriate boundaries around his food bowl but was not aggressive. Instead of lunging at people who tried to pet him, I taught him to go behind my legs. In times of stress, he retreats there now, without needing my praise. It's his safe spot. I respect this by not allowing people to follow him there. He is pretty darn cute. So, people want to look at him and pet him. Even though he has made awesome progress, behind my legs is off limits to anyone but Felix, his dog buddies, and myself.

Now, three years later, he does allow some people to pet him. Who gets to pet him is up to Felix. "The Gangster" still suits him well with some strange dogs. This label stuck and continued to make many people laugh.

Then I realized that sometimes Felix was proud to be a gangster! No joke! He had a big grin after his naughty behavior. Oh, no! By labeling him that, I was also creating it and allowing it to continue. So, I stopped and allowed a different behavior to emerge. Now, instead of attacking another dog or, when on leash, hiding behind my legs, he may come out wagging his tail and try to sniff them. Off leash, he may run away when an energetic dog runs by him, instead of biting the fur off the passerby's thigh. Felix is actually changing his personality. Sit with that one for a moment. Felix is changing his personality. I praise him for that all the time now.

I ask Felix what changed. He says, "I started to realize that I could be in the moment and see things for what they are. I started to realize that you want me confident, calm, and smart, and I feel like I am that inside. When I acted like "The Gangster", I was really a scared bully. It helps me when you visualize me being the dog you want me to be.

"I now know how to do that because I have done it with other behaviors, like learning tricks and meeting people. Life is safer and more fun than I originally thought.

"What helped me was when you started labeling me a "Peaceful Pup" because that helps me feel the energy of peace. I still do "Gangster" sometimes, but I try to stop myself when I feel myself moving in that direction. It feels good to be this new me."

Good boy, Felix!

By being more conscious of our own behavior, we can teach our animals to be more conscious of their own.

Wouldn't you rather have a "Peaceful Pup" than a "Gangster"? Are you open to your animal changing his/her personality? What would that look like for you and for them?

# What Makes
# Your Pet Happy?

People often request that I ask their animal, "What would make your life happier?"

There are some common answers from dogs and cats that are easy to integrate into our routine.

Dogs ask for big, grassy parks surrounded by trees. They want to play ball or frisbee, or just walk around the park to sniff. Some just want to picnic on a blanket in the shade. Dogs love the feeling of rolling on the grass. If they are old or sensitive, the cushion of the grass is good for arthritic bodies or toes that seem to drag.

They like walking near water. Even if they don't wade in or drink from the water, they like to be around it. Streams, ponds, oceans, big lakes — it doesn't really matter. The soothing noise and the sense of peace it creates is incredibly calming to them.

Animals live at a frequency closer to nature's. It is important for their well-being that we create time in nature for them. It is where they let go of stress and reset. It is where they feel closer to their true selves. If you have an indoor cat, open a window, and give them a comfortable window perch to hang out on. If you have an aggressive or fearful dog, find an empty park, and just hang out.

"BBQ food" is a big request, and so is "refrigerator food," which mostly consists of cheese, chicken, and deli meats. Deli meats are commonly referred to as "the slippery meat" or "the floppy meat." Sweet potatoes, pumpkin, broccoli, ice cream, bone marrow bones, bully sticks, and no-hides are also high on the list.

Small dogs and cats like a "bed on the bed." This typically is a donut bed on your bed so that they don't fall off or get kicked while you are sleeping. They also like these donut beds in cars. Small dogs and cats are also big fans of sweatshirts, robes, cashmere sweaters, and your softest blankets.

Dogs want to learn. They want to go to "learning school," "doggie lessons," "jumping camp," "trick-training school," "scent-dog training," "dance lessons," or "smart-dog training." They want their minds stimulated. They want to learn tricks, or, if they are naughty, they actually want to learn boundaries. They are proud of good "waits" and "stays" and will often tell me how good they are doing controlling themselves, even if you feel they have a lot of work to do! High-drive dog breeds like German Shepherds, Cattle Dogs, Border Collies, Labs, Malteses, and many other breeds and mixes are constantly asking me what their people are trying to teach them.

They ask this even when you don't think you are teaching them anything. They ask things like, "Why do they pull me on a walk and push me around them?" "What are they asking me to do when they kick their foot at me at the door?" "I don't understand when they move their arms around. What are they asking?" "When I go into a 'down,' how long am I supposed to be there for?" If you think your animals are stubborn and distractive, it might just be that you're confusing them, and you need to learn to be clearer. You probably have body-language signals that you don't even know you have. It happens to even the best trainers. I have had a few "A-ha!" moments with this over the years.

Cats want open windows, bird feeders, birdbaths, water fountains, music playing, wind chimes, tunnels, and access to closets or the garage. They want "string play" or time outside even if it is on a harness. Many want to be brushed. They like crumbled freeze-dried treats. They want access to the sun, so leave those shades open! They like massages down their back. They want extremely clean litter boxes. Clean bedding is high on the list, and so are clean windows, dishes, and water bowls! So, get to work, or hire a house cleaner designated to the pet areas!

Exercise is a big one for all the animals. They want more walks and play time. Even cats that don't seem very active want to play more. Geriatric dogs want more outings — even if they stroll for only a few minutes.

All animals love songs! They love when their people sing songs with their name in it. They don't care if you sing well or not. It's just that you are both happy when you are doing it.

My Chihuahua-mix Easter asked me the other day, "I love when you sing. How do you know so many songs?"

I told her, "Because I make them all up!"

She didn't care.

Now, go make your pets happier!

# Chapter 4

# THE AGING AND THE SICK

# The Power of Our Minds
# Can Create Miracles

We are all connected to a vast field of energy. This energy flows freely. Depending on the nature of our thoughts, this energy will either flow peacefully, manifesting all we wish for, or it will get obstructed and create a bit of chaos or manifest things that we do not truly desire. We have all witnessed it. Happy people seem to always be experiencing good things, and people who are sad or stressed keep getting presented with more opportunities to be worried. I have always been fascinated with the power of our minds.

From a young age, I had amazing intuition and could speak telepathically. During college, I studied Reiki and other hands-on healing arts. The basis for all of them is the same. Have a clear image in your mind of what you would like to happen, feel that feeling in your body as if it *were* happening in the present time, act on the guidance of the Universe and/or your intuition, and be grateful for the small and wonderful things in your life. It's an easy concept. If you look back at your life, I am sure you can find instances where this has been true.

As a child, I manifested a pony. In high school, I manifested the final goal to win our field-hockey championships. More recently, I manifested a summer rental in Bend, Oregon, that would happily take my *seven* indoor pets. Some of you may have manifested multi-million-dollar companies, your dream home, curing yourself of cancer, won a trip to an awesome destination, found yourself in healthy, happy relationships, and/or found and purchased the car or the perfect pet you had been obsessing about.

Some of you may find yourself in chaos at some point in your life. You're never happy at your job, you feel sick and tired, your partner cheats and lies, the weight won't come off, you're in debt, your animals don't listen, nothing ever works out. Simply, all of this comes down to how you feel about yourself and what you feel like you deserve. If you don't respect yourself, others won't respect you (that includes your naughty dog). Love yourself, take time to enjoy life and all its treasures, check and discipline your thoughts, making them as positive as possible, and watch how things begin to change. It is simple and miraculous.

This applies also to our relationship with our animals in many ways, but the one I want to discuss today is when your animal has been diagnosed with a serious illness. I have been fortunate in my life to witness hundreds, if not thousands, of animals cured of cancer or live out long, healthy lives with cancer in their body. My late Australian Shepherd, Stormy, was given six months to live, with tumors on his liver and adrenal glands. He lived an awesome four more years to 16! Maia, my late wolf hybrid, had cancerous tumors down her ear canal near her skull and, at first, undiagnosed Rocky Mountain Spotted Fever. I was told she might not live two weeks. She lived five more years to 15!

Animals have a way of seeing the positive in any given moment. They want to survive. They want to play, be happy, and roll in the grass. They want to go to green parks, walk around water, and eat hamburgers, chicken, and ice cream. They want to ignore their pain and concentrate on the feeling of lying in the sun or getting a massage. They naturally fall into a positive mind frame.

It hurts me to write this, but we can ruin that for them. When we are obsessing about death, suffering, and pain, that is what we attract. Animals easily pick up our thoughts and feelings. When they pick up our chaotic minds, their natural thought process of getting better or dying gracefully and peacefully are tainted with images and feelings of pain, suffering, and fear.

When we believe the Universe supports us and our animals, miracles happen. The right veterinarian or treatment may be offered to us. Prayers and healing support are offered, and our animals get healthier and happier. Be willing to receive guidance, and be open to witnessing a miracle.

I did this for Stormy and Maia. For Stormy, I found CBD oil and the right diet to keep his liver healthy. Who would have known he loved cantaloupe and pineapple so much! For Maia, a veterinarian from Texas filled in for a sick vet. He recognized the signs of Rocky Mountain Spotted Fever immediately and started her on treatment. My late cat, Joey, had a terrible, weeping, crusty rash all over his chin. I was told these rashes never heal in older cats, whose immune system is typically weak. I prayed. That night, a veterinarian came to me in a dream and told me to give him wheatgrass juice internally and on the skin. I did it, and, in three days, the rash was gone.

Sometimes animals are in the course of dying, and we have to accept that, but it doesn't mean that dying has to be painful. My friend's dog had a spleen tumor the size of a soccer ball. It's amazing that it never ruptured. He died peacefully in his older years.

Take the time to find peace within yourself. Believe that the Universe wants to support you and your animals. Change your panic and stress to peace and happiness. Breathe. Stay in that space, and allow yourself to imagine the feeling of health and happiness. The results may be incredibly fast, or they may take a month or two. Believe that you and your animals deserve to be happy and well. Remember to be grateful! Life is truly all about love and what we choose to create around us.

# Roxy Could Teach
# Us All a Thing or Two

Roxy is a petite, nine-year-old Shih Tzu dog. She is white with black markings on her ears, side, and elbow. She stares inquisitively at you with her cataract blue eyes, which is confusing because her luminous coat and adorable body make her look like a 10-week-old puppy.

Her person called me to talk with Roxy because "Roxy has been sick and is being diagnosed with different issues." One of the issues was diabetes, which has been extremely hard to control. Roxy's person wanted to know if she was suffering and if there is anything she could do to help Roxy.

These are the types of sessions I do all day long. When I talk via telepathy with animals, they send me their thoughts, images, and feelings in their body. Oftentimes, these feelings are so overwhelming to me that my body creates tears. My body is processing their emotions and actually crying their sadness. I might also get their intense stomach pain or ringing in their ears. I must admit, I was a little worried that my session with Roxy would elicit these kinds of feelings. But, boy, was I wrong! I had tears, but not from sadness.

Roxy starts the session with, "Can I ask you about healing my grandma? She should sit next to a vase of flowers." Roxy is talking about her person's mother, who loves gardening but has been sick and depressed. Roxy is trying to bring her passion back.

Then Roxy says, "I don't mind being blind because I can see some shadows, but what is really bothering me is the cramping in my legs, and, also, I have this feeling of yuckiness. I love cuddles, kisses on my face, and even daddy — I can feel his face up against me. I just feel love. I love life. I was thinking that I could get a stroller and we could go for a walk; I could be under blankets. I could smell the fresh air because the smell is so good, and maybe we could go to that corner park where I can feel leaves on the ground.

"Mom, please take no offense, but this food you are feeding me is your worst cooking yet (vet-prescribed canned food!). I don't like it very much. You know that special food that you eat at Thanksgiving? It's meat and creamy. I love the creamy (gravy!). I should be eating that.

"Also, you know that food — how do I say it? It comes from a man in a window. I think that may help me. (Drive-through Dunkin Donuts! She may be craving sugar because of the diabetes.)

"I want to tell my veterinarian, 'You are fired.' I want to say this because I feel like she doesn't know how to fix me. I need a veterinarian who knows how to fix me. I don't think she tries hard enough. She is not focused on my issue. She is like, "Poor Roxy ... next!" (Her person has been feeling the same way.)

"Maybe my mom's hairdresser knows a good vet. (Do all pet owners talk to their hairdressers about their pets?)

"I want another doctor who is compassionate and obsessed with pets. The doctor would say, 'You know, Roxy — I think you are pretty healthy. We just need to throw away your medicine and give you a new one that works perfectly.'

"Listen — all of you. I know you are worried, but I am not going to die because I have sass and no anger.

"I am going to tell God, 'You have to wait, because I am not ready.'"

Roxy reminds me that, when we are suffering, it's our attitude that matters the most. Think about others, have a good sense of humor, spend time doing things you love, be grateful for the good things, ask for help, weed out what is bad, have no anger, and create a vision for the future. Couldn't we all be a little more like Roxy?

# To Stroll or Not to Stroll

I started to use a stroller with my dog when my late Australian Shepherd, Stormy, started rambling slowly, like an old bear, with his elbows turned out. At about mile two, he stopped to stare at me and then lay down with a huff. I purchased the Novel-Jogger Doggy Ride Stroller, the deluxe off-road stroller that could be converted to a bike trailer. Stormy rode in style, with his adorable black head and white chest, peering out and smiling at everyone he saw. He barked at seagulls at the beach as we pushed him through deep sand and up to the water's edge. He watched sunrises and sunsets while being pushed up mountain fire roads and shared his love with thousands of people in towns and convention centers up and down the west coast. Several years into his strolling, as he aged, I had to prop him up with a pillow or open up the front, so his legs could stretch out. There is no doubt in my mind that strolling added years to his life. Instead of lying at home on a dog bed, staring at the walls, he was out exploring and eating snacks at restaurants. He died at age 16. His last strolling adventure was the day before, at his favorite grassy park.

Out in nature, I was confident pushing Stormy's stroller. "That is so cool," people would remark. But my introverted self was more self-conscious in town. "Oh, my gosh, Laura. I had to stop. I thought you had a baby."

"No, it's Stormy," I would reply, shrinking a little bit in embarrassment, thinking to myself, *Is this what women do when they don't have kids? Am I that crazy dog lady?* I gave myself a pass. I am the pet psychic. What do people expect?

These feelings came to pass as Stormy's social media fan club grew. "Ahh, Stormy," I would hear, along with the sound of car doors opening. Strangers with gleaming faces surrounded his stroller, showering Stormy with pets and love. He looked up at them with his big chestnut eyes and smiled for hundreds of selfies.

Cars drove by with children hanging out the windows screaming, "Hi, Stormy!"

One of my guy friends had no qualms about pushing Stormy in his stroller, and, when his dogs got old, they had strollers, too. I have sat in many living rooms of clients and suggested strollers for their aging or injured dogs. The husbands always stand up, roll their eyes, and pace a few steps. "I am not going to take my dog out in a stroller," they declare, emphasizing "Stroll-err."

The wife crosses her hands in her laps and looks at her dog with a grin — holding herself back from searching Amazon, I surmise.

A month later, I am emailed pictures of the husbands with big smiles on their faces, strolling the dog at the beach or posing happily with the dog in a stroller with a glass of wine at an outdoor restaurant.

"Thank you for convincing me to get a stroller," my friend says as we stand in line at a coffee shop. Her two small dogs are asleep in their stroller, sheltered by the cover. "People are much more understanding. They are happy that I have them contained. I take them into restaurants, stores, hotels, and coffee shops all the time. Living in New York City with the dogs is so much easier now. I am so glad I have them off the dirty street until we can get to the park."

A good stroller can be a monetary investment, but it is well worth the price. Ten years after its purchase, Stormy's stroller has strolled five other dogs — four until their passing and, presently, a rescue beagle as she loses weight until she can walk the full distance on her own.

Our egos often get in the way of living our lives more fully. Don't let your ego hold you back. Be happy and take the leap! Experience the joys of strolling with your dog.

# How Do Cats Feel About Being Declawed?

**2009 Article:**

I know a lot of cats that have been declawed. Before I was an animal professional, I didn't think much of it. When I was ten years old, a family friend gave us a large, orange, female tabby cat named Samantha. She had previously been an indoor-only, Park Avenue, New York City cat. When she came to our house, she became the barn cat. She was declawed, although that did not stop her. She could jump four feet in the air and grab a bird in flight and climb the ladder to the hayloft with ease. Dotti, another declawed cat, could hunt mice and climb trees.

A few years ago, I was called to a client's house to talk to three cats in the same home. Two had already been declawed, and one was scheduled for the following day. I was mortified and haunted by what they told me. They were in excruciating pain. It hurt to walk. They felt mutilated, traumatized, and upset with their person. The other cat was so frightened about what would happen to her the next day that she wouldn't come out from under the bed.

What I learned that day is that declawing a cat means the vet *amputates* part of the cat's paw! They cut off the last bone of the cat's toes! Take a moment to take this in. They actually cut off bone and nerves so that they don't scratch your furniture … Breathe. Do you understand? Do you know cats can feel pain and have emotions? Often vets send these cats home without painkillers. What? How is that legal and not animal abuse?

These cats are then in so much pain that they walk on their toes. I was sick for days, and, unfortunately, I could not convince the owner to stop declawing the other cat. It was one of those times that I could not "meet a person where they are" or have compassion for her. I felt she was abusive, and I found it hard to forgive her for getting the third cat declawed. I wanted to take all three cats away from her. I felt she didn't deserve them. I am still brought to tears at the memory of that session.

Let's hear it from cats that have been declawed:

## DOTTIE HAS BEEN DECLAWED

Dottie: "I was declawed because I ripped my person's favorite chair. I have never been in so much pain. I survived a coyote attack, and being in its jaws was nothing to the feeling I had when I woke up and noticed that I didn't have part of my paws. I hated my person so much afterwards that I ran away and found a new family."

## MAGIC HAS BEEN DECLAWED

Magic (recently declawed): "I couldn't swallow for weeks after my surgery. I was in so much pain that it was hard to breathe. I didn't understand it. I need my claws to climb. I think that, because I don't have my claws, my body doesn't work right. I can walk and play, but it feels different. My neck hurts a lot, and so does my back. I never thought people could be so mean. I hated my people so much that I kept biting them. They have been talking about giving me away to someone else. But then you came over and told me they didn't know any better — they didn't know it was cruel. You kept telling me how sorry you were for me. That made me feel better because you understand how terrible it felt. I knew that, if I were your cat, you wouldn't have declawed me. I wish you'd told my people earlier. I am learning to trust and love them now. I don't bite anymore, and they are going to keep me. I am learning to forgive them."

## SUSAN HAS BEEN DECLAWED

Susan (declawed the day after I told her people how the other cats felt about being declawed and how scared Susan was): "I felt so blessed that you came over and talked us all through it. I hate my person more than anything now. I can't stand to look at her. I try to throw up on her things as often as I can. I have a good life with my other cat siblings, but I hate my person so much that, at times, I wish she would stop breathing. Before this happened, I loved her more than anything. I would comfort her when she was upset, and I would try to be perfect. It didn't mean anything to her. If I had enough courage, I would run away. I feel like half a cat without my claws. I don't know if I could survive outside. I wish I had a different life. I wish I was brave enough to run away."

★ Reading this over, I am taken back by Susan's comment, "I wish she would stop breathing." Breathing is something a young animal doesn't really think much about. When someone is in pain, they often struggle to breathe. Susan wanted her person to experience more pain than she was in. It breaks my heart that humans' treatment of animals can create such a thought in an innocent creature's mind. Shame on the people who know that declawing is cruel and do it anyway.

## 2019 Addition

The above article was originally published in 2009. Reading over what the declawed cats said still brings me to tears. The animals' voices in this article are just three of so many that feel this way. Since this article was written, I have spoken to hundreds of other cats that have been declawed. Many had behavioral issues such as aggression, biting, and attacking as well as peeing and pooping outside the litter box and severe paw and back pain.

Some declawed cats are extremely sweet and are described by their owners as "fat and lazy." What these owners don't realize is that these cats are less active because of the intense nerve pain in their paws that they are experiencing when they walk.

Since my early 20s, I have been the proud person of six cats (Winston, Juliette, Joey, Makia, Serafina, and Ella). All of them wanted to scratch the furniture. With a little patience and some training, every single one of them learned not to scratch the furniture within a matter of a month or so.

If people take the time to be conscious and learn how to communicate with their pets more effectively, this issue of teaching cats not to scratch furniture is easier to train than teaching a puppy not to grab what they shouldn't.

If you have declawed your cat or have adopted a cat that has been declawed, there are a few things you can do make amends for the human cruelty they endured. Tell your cat that you are so sorry that either you or the people who declawed them were so unaware of the pain that it can cause. Tell them that you regret it and that people around the world are trying to stop animals from being declawed. Tell them that you love them and that you are going to make their body feel better. Often when cats have been declawed as kittens, their body can be out of alignment because of the distorted, uneven distribution of weight they bring to bear trying to avoid the pain in their paws. It is important to get them adjusted by a chiropractor and put them on CBD to help with inflammation and pain. Acupuncture can also help.

Learn to watch your cats' body-language signals when you pet them in order to notice if they are in pain and where. Mouth closing, body freezing, twitching of the tail, twitching of the skin, staring at you or in another direction, growling, biting, and getting up to leave are just a few behaviors animals will exhibit when they are uncomfortable. If your cats' skin twitches or rolls when you pet them down the back, chances are they have pain and have a pinched nerve.

Declawing cats is cruel. West Hollywood, San Francisco, Denver, Los Angeles, and all of New York state have already put a ban on declawing cats. So have much of Canada and all of these countries: England, Scotland, Wales, Italy, Austria,

Switzerland, Norway, Sweden, Ireland, Denmark, Finland, Slovenia, Brazil, and Australia.

# Healing a Sick Pet

In April of 2012, my 12-year-old Australian Shepherd Stormy (now passed) was diagnosed with tumors on his liver and pituitary gland, along with Cushing's disease. His black, shaggy fur fell out, leaving his coat orange and brittle. He drank a lot of water, was lethargic, and had a potbelly. I was told he had roughly six months to live. That was not OK with me. I put Stormy on CBD and Samè, lowered his protein, and increased his fruits and veggie intake.

Stormy lived four more years, dying at the age of 16. In that time, all of his shaggy fur returned. He was arthritic but healthy and vibrant, until one morning after breakfast, he looked at me and told me it was time. With the help of our vet, he died peacefully in the back of my '67 VW bus.

His miraculous healing was a testament to the power of living in joy. A month after his diagnoses, Stormy shared this wisdom on The Pet Psychic Radio Show:

> "My mom and I are healing me. I have something inside of me that I would rather not have. Don't worry. It's OK. It doesn't hurt. I pant and have soreness in my belly. I pretend it's not there. That's not

always the best idea because it can get worse. You have to do something. If your animal has an issue, or if you want to think about me in a healing way, think of your animal's body (or mine) working at its optimal performance. I eat healthy veggies, meat, supplements, and treats, but no grains.

"We picture a ball of light that looks like the sun, inside of my body, healing all my cells and organs. We say this affirmation: 'My body is well balanced and healthy. I believe in miracle healings. Thank you, Universe, for supplying all that we need to heal. I'm flexible and athletic. I have healthy teeth, gums, skin, and fur. I am well. I enjoy life to the fullest.'"

"An affirmation like this is important because it creates a pattern of health and fun all around you and your family.

"If you give your animal a new medication or supplement, you have to say this to them — but first take a deep breath, and remember to picture everything you say. 'This is the medicine I am going to give you (show them the medication). This medicine will make your body well. (Picture your animal really happy and well.)

"'If this medicine makes you feel bad in any way (picture them feeling yucky), exaggerate your symptoms, and look at me so I know something is wrong. If the medicine makes you pant a little, pant a lot, and look at me. If the medicine makes you dizzy, show me.' This is important. You want to know. Medicine hidden in food can cause fear and confusion in your animal.

"Then tell your animal, 'If the medicine makes you feel bad, we will try a lower dosage (picture less medicine), or we will try a different medicine (picture getting the other medicine). Then say to your animals, 'I believe that animals can be happy and healthy to the ends of their lives. I'm committed to making sure you're happy and healthy until you are ready to join all the angels and the essence of the Universe.'" (Picture whatever you think Heaven is).

"Tell them, 'I love you,' pet them, and go for a walk or play with them while saying your affirmation of health. You can sing these affirmations with your animal's name in it. That is what my mom does. We make up all sorts of healthy songs.

"Always remember, just because your animal is sick or has a bad diagnosis, it doesn't mean that you can't live in joy with your pet. It just means you need to be more active in achieving health, and you need to enjoy your time together more. All animals love treats. My mom and I wish you great health and a fun life. Remember, talking to your animal is helpful."

# Ailing Pets Come into Our Lives for a Reason

A woman named Mary called me from Latvia. She'd recently rescued three stray nine-month-old kittens. They were spayed and neutered and moved into an apartment she uses as a home for rescue cats until they get adopted. She does not live there. The kittens were quarantined in a large dog crate away from the other 10 cats, just in case they had any infectious diseases.

During the first 12 days, the kittens had been periodically throwing up. Mary assumed it was either because of stress from being in a new place and/or the recovery from surgery and anesthesia. She didn't think much of it. One morning, she found two kittens dead. For the next four days, Mary and her veterinarian tried to save the third kitten, but this kitten eventually died. They had feline distemper, a highly contagious, life-threatening viral disease, similar to the canine parvo virus.

Mary called me three months later. Her voice quavered on the phone. "I can't forgive myself. I must have done something wrong. If only I had taken them to the vet sooner," she cried. "If only I had not stressed them by putting them in that crate. If only I'd brought them to my house, they might still be alive today."

I tried to explain feline distemper to her, but she would not let the guilt go. Many times, it's not what I can say that helps people. It's what their animals say that helps them the most. We turned to the cats in Heaven.

> Kitty #1, a male, white with black spots, says, "We felt sick from when we were very small. We did get worse at her house, but it wasn't her fault. It was a warm, safe place. I felt feverish. You loved us. You were trying to make us happy. You have calm eyes and a sweet voice that made me feel safe. When we were in the cage, we slept. I wanted to move more, but I felt safe."

> Kitty #2, a male snowshoe, says from Heaven, "When I died, it was because an angel came for me. I was getting sick, and the angel said, 'I am going to lift you up.' When I was lifted up, I felt a sense of peace."

> Kitty #3, a female tuxedo, says from Heaven, "I didn't know about hospitals for cats. I didn't know about any of that stuff. So many people touched me with kind eyes and love in their hearts. I had a lot of love before I died. A lot of people wanted me to be well. When I was little, I felt troubled a lot. I had anxiety when the wind would blow. When we were inside, I found some peace. I thought,

*This is how we are supposed to feel.* When I died, I died in love. I can run now and spin and run in another direction. I couldn't do that before. My dizziness is gone."

Often in my work, people come to me to speak to animals that they had in their care only for a little while. I believe these animals come to us to die. There is a force that brings these people and animals together so that an animal that has been neglected, abused, or unknown can feel a sense of love and safety before they die. This feeling of love helps these animals to cross over into a higher dimension of ecstasy or comfort.

Often, people are cruel to themselves and dwell on issues like, "Why did my animal have to die? Why do I have to witness this suffering? I can't stand it. Am I being punished? I must have done something wrong. It's all my fault."

It pains me to witness this. These people have been chosen by a loving force field or by an angelic dimension to teach these animals that people can love them and fight for them, and that this world is a loving, safe one. To die with that knowledge and that feeling is an incredible gift. These people should hold their heads high, with their hearts wide open, and be proud that they were able to be of such service. The Universe chose them in particular for their embodiment of love and compassion. If these people are able to understand this, then they are honoring not only the life of that animal but also a divine mission that they have fulfilled.

# The Best Medicine
# for Your Pet?
# Pawsitive Energy

I f your animal is diagnosed with an "incurable" disease or has a behavior issue that is less than desirable and you want to change it, your attitude is the most important. If you find yourself obsessing over a negative outcome or replaying past events, the situation is only going to get worse. Your animal is going to feel your stress and become more anxious. This may increase the symptoms of their illness or force them to act out with their behavior.

That's right. It's all your fault. I am joking. It's not *all* your fault, but you do have the power to create a better future for you and your pet. You can remain a victim and replay the problems in your head, or you can take a deep breath and decide what changes are needed to be made in order to get your animal well, support them in their transition to Heaven, or to rehabilitate their behavior.

If they are sick, of course, educate yourself on their illness, and look into alternative methods of healing. If they have a behavioral problem, look into humane, non-forceful ways to train them. It's equally important to pay attention to your mind and the thoughts that you are putting out there. What you think and feel is what you create. Animals, by their instinctual nature, know this. When we are looping our minds in chaos, it taints our animals' well-being. Reading your thoughts, feelings, and energy comes naturally for animals, so you'd better be careful. Your negativity could be making them worse. But your positivity could be fueling them into great health and right actions.

"Easier said than done," you might be saying. I get it. I have been there. Stormy, my late Aussie, was diagnosed with Cushing's Disease, and liver and pituitary tumors. He was given less than six months to live. Maia, my wolf-hybrid, had cancerous tumors in her ear canal connected to her skull, and it was expected that she had less than two weeks to live. Makia, my cat with a spleen tumor and diabetes, was given months to live. All these animals lived well for another four to eight years, dying at 16, 15, and 21 years old. What did they do, naturally? Live like they weren't sick, finding joy in the moment. Stormy played and smiled with every person and dog he saw. Maia ran wild in the woods and stuck her head out the car window, and Makia saw herself as beautiful and climbed up the roof of the house until days before she died. They felt joy and knew that, when it was time to die, they would be entering the dimension that gave them energy and happiness all along. They were brave and full of love. This is what our animals want out of life. Fine — give yourself a pity party and curl up on the couch, but, the next morning, conjure up happiness, and really play. Watch your lives change.

*"If you feel yourself being negative, you have to remember that love is big. Love is bigger than all of us. And if you can find a little bit inside of you and concentrate on that, eventually you'll feel the enormity of it."*

— STORMY, 5/23/2013

*"Love is a stream of consciousness. If you connect into that stream and anchor yourself to it, you will always be protected. Love is following what is true. Love is being honest about what you can or cannot do. Love is believing in yourself to accomplish what others may think is impossible. When you love an animal or person fully, it helps them reside in the stream of love. Heaven has many different dimensions. Love runs through all of them. The highest dimension is pure love. I reside there."*

— MAIA FROM HEAVEN, 2/15/2012

*"Love is easy if you let go of resistance. Make joy a priority. I don't know how long I'm going to live. Don't be scared of losing me. Enjoy the time with me."*

— MAKIA, 3/5/2012

# The Most Difficult Decision for a Pet Owner

Deciding to euthanize your animal is often a painful decision. Everyone wants to know, "How will I know?" This is a tough question for any animal owner. Some animals can endure an enormous amount of suffering and still enjoy life, while others feel only a little pain and are ready to transition. Unless you are in an emergency situation and the decision is made for you, ultimately the decision is up to you and your animal. I always know the time is close when my animal's pain outweighs their joy. I rely on my animals to tell me when this is the case.

You don't have to be a pet psychic to be able to understand your animal when they are ready to give up and cross over. If you are open to the concept of euthanasia and to hearing from your animal that they are ready to go, you will just know. Your animal will tell you, and you will feel it strongly in your heart that the decision has been made. Without a doubt, you will move forward with making the arrangements.

Often after the animal has passed away, people have what I call "euthanasia guilt" and forget how strongly they felt while making that decision. They feel like they played God. But this is not so.

Knowing when it is time is really about trusting your own intuition about how your pet feels and not doubting it later. This can be tricky, because the end is not always the debilitating suffering that we expect it to be.

I'll sometimes hear, "I'll know when my dog stops eating. He loves to eat." Sometimes this is true, but not always. My late Aussie, Stormy, ate his favorite eggrolls, homemade by a friend, up until an hour of his passing.

Sometimes before an animal passes, they have a surge of energy that allows them to engage in some of their favorite pastimes. People often think their animal has turned a corner to wellness, but, in actuality, it's a welcoming surge before the decline.

Another comment I hear all the time is, "One day I think it's time, and the next day I don't. I don't trust myself to make this decision." The reason this is happening is because your animal is also on the fence. One day they feel pretty good and are telling you they can hang on. The next day, they feel pretty terrible and think it is probably time to go. I told my late wolf-dog Maia she had to tell me three days in a row before I made the decision. I needed to see that look in her eyes for three days, and it's OK if you need that, too.

It is important to be aware of whom to talk with during this difficult time. Be selective about whom you share your story with. Some people are just not animal people. They don't understand that we love our animals like children. You don't need to justify your decisions with these people. Spending time doing so will only make you frustrated.

They may see your animal topple over when they walk or see that they are blind. They may hear that you are giving them fluids every day and think you're crazy. "Just put them down and out of their misery" is something you may hear. Find compassionate animal people for support. There are many wonderful online groups that show up — sometimes surprisingly — to support people during this process. You may have a good friend, a pet-sitter, or a veterinarian technician who becomes an angel for you and your animal.

At this time, it is important to have moments of silence to allow guidance and your animal's thoughts and feelings to permeate through your consciousness.

Spend some time telling your animal what you feel about the afterlife and that *you* will be OK if they go. Tell then that you don't want them to suffer any more than they have to. I tell them they will still remember us and will be able to visit us. I tell them that people who know us on the other side will come for them, like our ancestors and deceased friends and close family members. These people do not need to know our pets in life in order to take care of them in Heaven. I tell the animals that they will feel young in body and retain all the wisdom they gained in this life. They will be able to do everything they love. So, it's OK if they no longer want to stay here.

I tell them, when they are ready, to stare a family member in the eye and tell them over and over again that they want help or to talk to their people in the middle of the night, so their people will wake up with a knowing awareness. The animals will do this act naturally. Often people say to me, "I just knew.

I just looked at him or her and knew." Or "I woke up and just knew it was the day."

You have to trust in this. Most of the time, it's the animal's decision — not the people's. The people just hear them and carry out their wishes.

Unfortunately, in times of dementia or during a physical emergency, you need to make that decision without the animal's consent. When this happens, the animals usually tell me from Heaven, "I have always been taken care of. I trust them. They made the right decision."

If you doubt your decision afterwards, it blocks your ability to feel your animal from the other side. Your psyche is too cluttered with guilt to feel your animal's love around you.

Other times, I have seen animals tell their people over and over that they want to go, but the people are not ready to let them. The animal suffers unnecessarily because their person doesn't want to "feel like 'God'" or live without their animal. I understand this. I don't judge these people because it's their path, and some animals die very peacefully naturally.

But I urge you to really think about this and to contemplate and wonder, *Am I open to helping my animal cross over if they don't want to fight anymore?* If so, talk with your animal about it, and then let it go. When the time is right, your animal will tell you. I am sure of it.

After you have helped them go, mourn your loss, and be open to sensing the beauty of how your animal feels in the afterlife. There will still be a connection, and, if you are open to receiving it, you will feel it.

# Chapter 5

# DEATH — THE OTHER SIDE OF AIR

# Jinx: A Christmas Story

I was home from college. It was Christmas morning 1992. Jinx, my childhood white-and-black English cocker spaniel was old, mostly blind and deaf, and was acting more distant toward me. I would go to cuddle him and he would pull away. I sensed he was jealous that I'd brought my German Shepherd home and that my brother had brought his Labrador. I took Jinx outside for some one-on-one time. I didn't "consciously" talk to animals back then, but I knew what they were thinking and feeling. He sat down in the snow. I squatted beside him, putting my arm around him. When he leaned away from me, I got an overwhelming feeling that he was ready to leave this world.

"Oh, buddy," I said. "You have been the best dog ever. I will miss you so much." He leaned against me, licked me on the cheek, and then nuzzled his nose and neck into my shoulder. Tears were streaming down from my eyes. I knew at that moment that I was saying goodbye. Love poured down between us. After a few minutes, my father caught sight of me wearing the shorts and t-shirts I'd slept in. He said, "Get inside, and put on some clothes. It's freezing out here." I took a moment and kissed Jinx. He understood. I would see him in a bit.

Less than an hour later, the family was sitting in the dining room having Christmas breakfast when I caught sight of Jinx standing in the doorway between the kitchen and the dining room. His tail was wagging, his eyes were bright, and his head was erect. I took a fresh breath, feeling amazed that he might be with us a little while longer. I was overwhelmed with joy at the sight of him. That moment is so crystal clear to me.

Ten minutes after that, my brother left to go pick up his girlfriend at the train station. My eyes followed my brother out. Through the dining-room door, I could see the glass kitchen door leading to the outside. He shut it behind him. Suddenly he turned to get back in. There was extreme terror on his face. Frantically, he pulled on the doorknob. It was locked. Speechless, he waved his arms in alarm.

I knew right then that Jinx was dead. I don't know how I knew it, but I did. My father had never brought him back inside. The breath emptied out of me. My father, knowing what I knew, hurried to the outside. "Don't come out here!" he screamed back to the family as he opened the door. I didn't listen. I ran outside. Jinx was lying motionless on the driveway with my dad hovered over him. Jinx's cataract blank eyes were rolled back. The tie-out line he must have been tied to was unraveling. It was spinning in coils from its line. That was before dog tie-out lines had swivels on them.

"Holy sh★t! He hung himself," I screamed.

"No, he didn't," my father lied. He was trying to protect me.

"Did he commit suicide, or was it an accident? I thought you'd brought him inside!" I screamed.

My father couldn't look at me. It took him 12 years to tell me the truth. The image of that line uncoiling is etched in mind, but not as vividly as seeing Jinx's spirit smiling at me and wagging his tail in the doorway at breakfast. He had crossed over and had come back to let me know he was OK.

That night I took out the stationery I'd received for Christmas and wrote Jinx a letter. I told him how grateful I was for our life together. He'd been my hiking and jogging companion, coming to my sports games and even accompanying me on some late-night sneak-outs, among many other things. I told him I loved him and would never forget him.

After I finished the letter, my hand would not stop writing. I started to write a letter from Jinx to myself. It spoke of running alongside my horse's legs with me on trail rides, sharing my Pepperidge Farm cookies and bagels with cream cheese, dropping me off at the school bus when we were young, the time my best friend, Robby, and I married our dogs in his mother's rose garden. I was reminded of the time Jinx protected me from a fight with my teenage brother. Jinx jumped on my brother, pushing him into the pool. I wrote about morning snuggles and how I would cry into his fur. I was reminded of teaching him how to jump the horse jumps and hanging out with the bunny.

Little did I know that that letter would be the first of thousands of channelings and writing about what animals tell their people. If you have a phone session with me today, you will hear me typing the thoughts and feelings of your animals as they come through. It was Jinx who brought that alive for me.

People are always sad when their animals die on significant dates. But I am glad Jinx died on Christmas day. This way, no matter how many years pass, he will always be in my heart on Christmas day.

# Lala's Passing

Lala looked like a small, 50-pound German Shepherd, but a DNA test revealed her to be a German Shepherd-coyote cross. The owners of my hometown gas station adopted her from a high kill shelter. They went looking for a guard dog. Lala tried to attack them while they were walking by her kennel — and then became their fast friend as soon as they opened the door. What I know about Lala now is that this was a conscious decision on her part. She didn't bite them, because she'd picked them.

They named her "Tequila" because she was "unpredictable." Tequila quickly became known as "Tequil-lala" or "Lala" by all who knew her. Problems arose when she started biting the butts of unsuspecting customers. My guy friends who pumped gas there giggled like middle-school girls behind the office window every time Lala got into her crouching position. Lala would execute her bite and then come trotting into the office with her head and tail held high in pride. Whoever was closest to the mini-fridge opened it up and handed her a piece of bologna. Clearly, she was being trained to bite, but they had not figured this out. The owners started to chain her so that she wouldn't scare off customers or get them sued.

One night, driving home, I spied Lala huddled behind the soda machine, with her two front paws and nose just sticking out from behind it. She was trying to keep warm against the bitterly cold and windy New York night. I was angry. My friends lived above the gas station. I was furious. How could they leave here out like that?! Didn't she usually sleep inside? I was in twelfth grade at the time. I was confused. Didn't people realize that Lala had feelings? That she can get cold? This was before cell phones and the internet. I didn't know about animal abuse or animal rescue, or, for that matter, about anyone fighting for animal welfare. I look back at that time and wonder if it was just my world that was unconscious. I lived on a horse farm and showed my horse every weekend. No one spoke about the thoughts and feelings of animals. I didn't understand how that could be. There was love for animals, but it was different from how people love now.

It was a shock to my boss and the gas station guys that Lala never tried to bite me. My friends who lived above the station would dare me to sneak through the window to see if I'd be attacked. Lala just looked at me, wagged her tail, and stuck by my side so I would pet her. She never tried to hurt a child either. I babysat the owner's young children. They would climb all over her, pulling her fur and tail and sticking their fingers in her ears. All the while, Lala either lay quietly or licked their faces. I started to unchain her and take her with me every time I had the kids. Lala and I started to form a strong bond. She listened to my every word and never left my side. Each time I had her, it was harder for me to place her back on the chain until one day, I just didn't. There was something so strong in me that told me it just wasn't an option anymore. I loved her and I didn't want to be separated from her. My bosses never fought me on this. They loved her too. They knew a chained life was no life for a dog and they wanted what was best for her. That day, I brought her into my parents' house. My mother chased us out. "Laura, get that dirty dog out of here. I see her lying all over that filthy gas station."

I knew that only a professional grooming would satisfy my mom, so I drove Lala straight to the local dog-grooming shop. Lala went in looking like a black German Shepherd and came out with beautiful, reddish-golden color fur. People thought she was a red wolf after that. I recognized her only because she was jumping all over me, whining and prancing all over the shop like she was the most gorgeous dog alive. From that day, we were inseparable.

After a few weeks, we got on a flight so I could go back to college in Boulder, Colorado. I knew nothing about training a dog for traveling in a crate or about the dangers of flying. I just showed up at the airport, bought a crate there, and put her in it. My whole life with Lala was like that. I needed her to do something, so she did it. I often look back at that time in my life, and I wonder if my clients (and even myself at times) baby their animals too much and give them excuses to act fearful. Sometimes, you just need faith that it will work out — so just do it.

Lala was the kind of dog that never needed training or a leash. She was just perfect from the start. She was never far from my heels, and, because I stopped praising her for biting, she basically stopped biting people — except people who deserved it but those are stories for another time. No matter where I left her, she stayed. She never needed a fence and never roamed farther than the property line of where I left her. And I left her many strange places — my parents' house, multiple friends' houses, dorm rooms, strange cars with the windows all the way down, and outside of stores. She just knew I would return.

She was smart. One time, my friend, Craig, took her and another dog on a long hike up a mountain. In three hours, they were at the top of the mountain, and Lala and the other dog saw some elk and took off after them. The other dog came back, but Lala did not. My friend stayed on the mountain for hours, calling her, but a snowstorm came and he had to retreat back down. At the trailhead, he waited in the car to see if she would return. When I got home from work, seven hours after her disappearance, my friend met me at the door in tears. "I lost her. I am so sorry."

"Where were you?" I asked.

He told me which mountain.

"Did you go by the old house?" I questioned.

"No, that is miles and miles away. We were at the trailhead on the other side of the mountain. She probably doesn't even know it's the same mountain."

"Yeah, she does." I just had faith that she would go back to the old house at the base of that mountain. A year had passed since we'd lived there, but I knew she would remember. We hopped in the jeep. When we drove into the driveway of our old house, there she was, lying on the front stoop.

A man heard us pull up. He came out the front door and said, "I kept shooing her away and she just kept coming back and lying on the stoop. She had no interest in me. Just the stoop. So, I fed her some bologna, gave her some water, and figured she knew what she was doing. I trusted that someone would show up for her. And here you are. How strange. That is one smart dog." I question these days, "Did she ask for that bologna?"

Lala leaped all over me whining and then jumped in the jeep to give Craig kisses. He cried with relief.

Lala and I lived the life. We traveled all over the country together. We camped on beaches, in mountains in the middle of the wilderness, swam in rivers, oceans, and lakes, and slept at friends' apartments in cities. She went to college classes with me and to college parties. We were never separated. I felt extremely safe with her. I never worried about anything. It is the same feeling that some of my girlfriends talk about when they talk about their loving husbands: since they have been together, the world seems more joyful, loving, and safe. That is how I felt with Lala.

Lala was obsessed with three things. 1) Me. She never let me out of her sight. 2) Bees, which she loved to catch and eat (never to be stung) and 3) Rocks. Perhaps she never had toys as a pup. With rocks, she repeatedly kicked them with her two front paws toward her rear paws while backing up for many steps, or she kicked them with her front paws and spun her body around to catch it. She dove for them deep into water like a seal, Lab or Golden Retriever. She gnawed on them, grinding down her all teeth. She found "special ones" on hikes which she was determined not to leave.

Often, she carried them only for a certain distance, either because of their weight or because of their shape. The only times she ever ignored me was when she was obsessed with one of these rocks. She would lie next to it and refuse to leave it until I either picked it up and put it in my backpack or carried it with my bare hands. Although I tried many times, I could not trick her by carrying it a short distance and quietly putting it down. She would spin back around as if she had eyes in the back of her head and trot back to where I laid it, staring at me with an evil glare and then whining as she tried to put it back into her mouth or until I picked it up again. With great attention, she made sure that rock made it into the car. As you can imagine, at home we had an amazing rock garden. One of them I still have today, 28 years later.

I never saw Lala act the way she did with rocks with anything else until she did this behavior with a cat in a crate at the pet store. She would not leave her. So, I adopted Juliette then and there. Lala and she became best friends.

We met a guy, adopted another cat, Joey, moved to California, where I started a pet-sitting/dog-walking business while I was studying to be a T-Touch practitioner/animal trainer. Lala came with me on most of my pet-sitting walks, and, even though she had hip problems, she still let my two-year-old neighbor snuggle up with her and fall asleep.

I brought Lala to one of my weeklong Tellington-Touch training classes. There she watched me work with other animals. One of the trainers came over to me while I was working with a fearful black Lab mutt. Lala was close by, lying peacefully by my side. She didn't have the disposition to be jealous. She knew she was number one. This trainer told me that I had something special with animals. She noticed that animals were different with me than they were with other people and she wanted to know what I knew about that. "What are you doing?" she asked.

This was the first incident that was a catalyst to my figuring out what my relationships with animals are. I was in awe that someone noticed that I had something special with animals. I was just being me — *and* I was being "shy me." If people weren't watching, I would have been even more connected. That night I asked myself, *Am I different from other people? Does this explain why I don't understand so much of the way most people treat and view animals? Am I supposed to help people treat animals better? If someone I look up to is asking me what I am doing, does that create a responsibility to figure it out and teach others one day?*

I don't remember my response to this woman. I probably just shrugged and stroked Lala. But her comment put a fire in me that is still burning to this day. When I got home that week, I registered for an animal-communication workshop with Carol Gurney.

I believe in divine timing, but I didn't know this back then. The coincidence of what happened next sometimes makes me wonder. The day I came home from my first class with Carol, I was eager to try out what I'd learned with Lala. I called Lala up on the bed, stroked her, looked her in the eye, centered myself, and asked her, "Lala, how are you feeling today?"

She reached her out her golden-fur paw and touched my hand, looked me in the eye, and said, "Mom, I am dying inside."

Tears welled up in my eyes. "What?!" I didn't want to believe it. "Lala, you are doing so well. I know you are older, but you are still coming on the walks with me, and you are eating well. You are doing so well."

She didn't say anything, but she moved closer to me and put her head up against my chest and under my chin.

I called my boyfriend into the room and, through tears, told him what had happened. "You are not doing it right," he said. "That is just your biggest fear. She's not dying. I am sure she didn't say that."

But I wasn't convinced. I'd heard it too clearly.

Three days later, before I went to work, I said goodbye to Lala in the carport. She pushed her muzzle and head in between my legs, like she had done thousands of times before, and wagged her tail while I scratched her butt. When she backed up to look up at me, her eyes looked a little dull. When I came back eight hours later, she was lying in the carport, lethargic and almost unresponsive. My neighbors and boyfriend told me they never saw her move. I was mad at my boyfriend for not noticing she was sick or for not doing anything about it, but I never dealt with that. She spent that night in the emergency room getting blood transfusions.

I didn't know then what I know now. That's not good.

I transferred her to another hospital. There I was told she had tumors on her spleen and that she was bleeding internally. I am not the kind of person who can be scared easily, but, at that moment, I was filled with terror. My fingers actually went numb, and I thought I was going to faint. I didn't want to lose her. I didn't know if I could enjoy life without her. "She has to be euthanized, right now," one of the veterinarians said sternly. "It is the most humane thing to do. Those tumors can burst and inflict more pain."

I couldn't swallow. I remember thinking, *What do I do?* I have this memory as if I am outside of my body, my consciousness at the corner of the room, watching myself deal with this trauma. I see myself standing tall, chin up, and thinking, *What the "f" do I do? And who the hell can I call? I am not going call my boyfriend. I don't have anybody.* I felt completely alone even though I was surrounded by professionals I should have been listening to. And then, seemingly from outside of myself, from somewhere else in the Universe, I remembered that I read somewhere in a book to trust your own feelings and to advocate for your own animal. I wondered, *Am I being divinely guided?*

My next memory is of me watching myself with Lala. I sat in her kennel, stroking her with her head on my lap. I was being stared at by three vets through the glass windows. I asked Lala, "I don't know what to do. They think I should help you to Heaven now. What do you want? I will do whatever you want." Tears were streaming down my eyes. I didn't necessarily hear her words, but I was overcome with the intense feeling that she wanted to die at home with her cats.

I was very shy back then. It took a lot of internal strength to tell the vets I was taking her home. I knew it was what I had to do, and no one could convince me otherwise. They advised against it, shaking their heads in disapproval, but, as I was leaving, a woman vet came over to me and told me that she would have made the same decision and that, if Lala didn't pass during the night, she would come to the house to euthanize her.

Lala, the cats, and I had a beautiful night saying goodbye. We slept all together on Lala's dog bed next to an open door, periodically gazing up at the stars. Lala was calm and peaceful. That night, we talked about our life together, and I soaked up every feeling of her physical body. I never wanted to forget the way her fur felt in my hands or the way she smelled. She snuggled up against me, doing the same. In the morning, I knew it was time to call that vet.

When she arrived, we were out in front of my barn apartment, lying on the grass. The fog from the ocean had just receded. The sunlight was warm and comforting. I thought I would die with Lala. I had never been been present for a euthanasia, and I was scared but confident. I knew it was time. The vet explained what would happen. I hugged and kissed Lala, telling her to come and visit me and that I would love her forever. I don't think she was scared. She felt so ready.

When the vet gave her the shot, I just started to cry. Not that wailing kind of cry, but a truly present, deep sorrow, tears streaming down my eyes cry. Then everything just got silent. I didn't hear the birds or see the vet or my boyfriend. I was in some type of void where time stops. And then all of a sudden, I felt Lala and me in our greatest times deep in the wilderness. Then a charge of energy rose from my core to my heart and lingered there, expanding outward. I breathed her in, and I knew that she was inside of my heart and showing me the profound love and peace of the Universe, stretching out farther than the oceans, over the mountains, and into the stars. With every breath, it became more miraculous. Then the energy pulled out of my body, leaving me with tingles from head to toe; then it flickered in the atmosphere in front of me. It was like the way the sun reflects off water or the way the Colorado fall Aspen leaves flicker in the wind, and then she disappeared. I was left with such an ecstasy of love and joy that I could no longer feel sad. I felt amazing. I looked at the vet. She had her stethoscope on Lala, listening to see if she could hear Lala's heartbeat. She confirmed that Lala was dead. I looked at her and said, "She's gone."

I will never forget the look in the vet's eyes when she lifted her head to look at me. She looked shocked; then her eyes brightened, and she smiled. "Yes, she's gone," she said, stroking Lala's body. She didn't tell me, but I know she saw something beautiful in me at that moment. I could tell by the look of wonderment in her eyes.

My neighbor's little boy came running out of his house calling "Lala" and curled up with her body, hugging her like one does a Teddy Bear. "Is she sleeping?" his parents asked.

"No, she's gone," I said.

"She looks so peaceful. I thought she was sleeping," they said, letting their little boy say goodbye.

I had experienced a miracle in that moment with Lala. She gave me a glimpse of Heaven that would end up being my compass as I helped many rescue dogs into their transition at high kill shelters and helped thousands of clients through the death-and-dying process.

It has been more than 25 years since Lala's death, and I have felt that exact feeling only four other times. Trust me, I am not a stranger to feelings of miracles and bliss. I have had many mystical experiences in my life that would astound anyone into believing in the incredible workings of the Universe. The experience of Lala's passing was extra special.

I know that the divine orchestrated the timing of these earlier events so that I could be the person I am today — and so that I could help others have a more conscious bond with their animals and with the Universe.

I have learned that when we calm our internal chatter and follow the guidance that comes to us during the silence, the Universe opens up opportunities to support what is right for us. The more we trust in this, the more we will see it in our lives. I was blessed to have that animal trainer speak to me the way she did; to have had Carol's class at just the right time; to remember what was written in that book; to have that vet come to my home. They were all incredible gifts. I learned that I was not alone through it all, even though, at the time, I felt I was. This is a true blessing to remember in times of hardship.

My friends and family were shocked that I was not depressed after Lala's death. I was happy that she was out of a pain body and that she still exists somewhere. I couldn't feel sorry for myself for losing her, because I knew she would always be around me.

It is up to each of us to remain present, to listen to our internal compass, and to give credit to the miracles. Don't ignore them. Most of all, give thanks for divine presence in our lives. The more we do, the more we will recognize it when it's around us.

# What Animals Have Said After They Died

A regular part of my business is speaking with animals that have crossed over. I always love to hear what the first thing is that they say to a pet psychic when I contact them in Heaven. Here are a few:

Rogue, a two-year-old female tortoise-shell cat, said, "When I went to Heaven, I chased the moon. You know how it gets big? I chased it like a cat ball toy. I rolled over on my back and played with a man and his hands. The man is a father figure, like daddy; he has big eyes like daddy, and he has a kind heart."

> Her person writes: "My baby girl Rogue passed away on a warm summer night, around 9:00 p.m., as it was getting dark out, with my husband and me next to her. ... She was the quirkiest and funniest girl ever, and I am happy to know that she is back to her old self! I used to get depressed and would cry so much thinking about her, how she suffered, and how she had to leave this world so young. But,

whenever I get sad thinking of her, I just picture how happy she was to leave her disease-ridden body. She is restored. Indeed, when my little girl went to Heaven, she did chase the moon."

Shelby, a Shih Tzu who died at eight years old, said, "I cuddle in my mommy's chest at night. I haven't disappeared. Sometimes I run ahead and look back waiting for you to catch up to me."

> Her person writes: "These are things that Shelby would do all the time with us before she transitioned. It's wonderful to know she is still here with us."

Shelby also says, "Sometimes I ride in my Daddy's lap in the car and look out the window. I'm not afraid anymore."

> Her person writes: "Our precious Shelby loved her car rides, but she never liked to sit by the window because it made her nervous. When I heard her tell Laura this in our session, it broke my heart, but it also made me happy for her."

Jimmy, a German Shepherd, died at 10 years old. He said, "I want my mom to know that it is so cool here in Heaven. There is this place where I can go walking. There are all these trees that weep over me. We have so much fun. I have this grandpa man here who takes me on a boat. We are laughing. I get a lot of steak meat here in Heaven, and I live near a BBQ.

I want my mom to know that, here in Heaven, I can jump up on her bed. I can run really fast, and my body doesn't hurt at all anymore. I was so grateful when she set me free."

> His person writes: "I always loved taking Jimmy camping with me because I knew he loved it so much. Heaven for Jimmy sounds like our little vacation trips together: boating, walking, the barbeque, and sleeping together."

Sometimes our animals travel to Heaven in smells. One dog traveled in the smell of roses. Her person had an award-winning rose garden. Another dog traveled to Heaven in the smell of breakfast meats. His person made bacon almost every morning. Often, they are greeted by our friends or our ancestors. Our animals always have someone to take care of them. It is important to remember that they are happy and watching over us. If you can be open to that concept, then you will most likely feel your animals' spirits when they come to visit you.

# Are Pets Lonely
# in Heaven?

In my business, I speak to several people a day whose animals have passed away. People are always wondering if their animals are lonely on the other side. Not only do these animals mention being greeted by other animals during their passing, but they are often met also by people. More often than not, these people are friends, family members, and sometimes even distant ancestors of ours. These spirit people did not need to know our animals in life in order to greet our animals on the other side. They may not even have liked animals in their lifetime. These people come for our animals because they love us. They want to take care of the animal that we held dear. They want to feel us within our animals' souls. Some even want to make amends by doing for our deceased pets what they didn't do for us. Some deceased people show up during a session so that we know that their consciousness is still alive and that they are aware of what we are doing here in this realm.

This concept is so confusing for clients that it may take some time for people to recognize who exactly was brought up during the session. Some people know exactly who the person is meeting their pets. While others may take a day or two to realize that it was their own deceased sister that was described. Emails of wonderment are common in the weeks after a session.

There are a lot of dogs getting picked up and being driven around Heaven in classic cars and old pickup trucks. Some are riding in Mustang convertibles, baby-blue Fords, Bentleys, and Cadillacs. Some even talk about the interior color and design of the cars. One dog was riding around in the sidecar of a motorcycle.

I hear from clients, "That is the kind of car my mom and dad had. My dad would never let our family dog in the car! He was scared the dog would scratch the interior." "My grandpa loved that old pickup. I used to ride in it when I was a kid." "My best buddy always said he wanted to have a sidecar for his dog."

There are not only car rides in Heaven, but also lots of food. I have heard from deceased animals, "I am with the grandma who loves the cannoli." "A sister figure with long red hair is feeding me cut-up meat on special flowered plates." "I'm on a boat with your friend; we are eating hamburgers, and he is drinking lots of beer."

My clients respond, "Oh, my gosh! My mom loved cannoli." "My great-aunt used to have those plates." "That is my brother. He loved beer, his boat, and hamburgers."

Cats are walking in "safe gardens," hunting without killing, and sleeping on our ancestors' knitted blankets, while dogs are running in great green parks with our relatives and friends. Many animals are sitting on the laps of our deceased friends and family members, watching TV. These people are doing what we did with our pets, mirroring our lives so that our animals feel at home.

Sometimes our ancestors use our animals to tell us something important. A deceased cat says, "Your father says to check the foundation. There is a leak there. Take care of it." Yes, my client already knew. She had been debating whether to get it fixed or not.

A dog says, "Your sister says to be brave and go back to school." That client never told anyone her dreams about getting her master's degree.

Then there are even bigger surprises. When a deceased dog says, "There is a child here with me who is now a grown man. He says that he helped with the keys." The day after that session, I got an email from a client saying that her sister had lost a one-year-old boy in 1991 and that, the day before our session, her sister found some keys that had been lost for a long time.

I believe in divine timing. I wondered: *Did the boy help her find her keys so that she could get the message during our session — so that she could believe he still exists somewhere?*

Sessions connecting people with their deceased pets are a constant reminder that we are not alone and that we have support from invisible forces. We are never left by the ones that pass away. I find great comfort in this.

From Heaven, a Husky dog named Maxwell said to me, "I eat good here. There is a stew meal that is really delicious. I am with a man who reminds me of dad." Maxwell's people, a husband and wife, had no idea what the stew was. They said they had never fed Maxwell stew or even eaten stew them-selves. The husband's father was still alive, and his grandpa died when he was young. Dave asked, "Why would my grandpa be with my dog?"

Although I see ancestors with our pets all the time, I told them to ask the husband's dad to see if he knew what the stew was. What the animals mention are not random. With some thinking and investigating, it usually makes sense. Details can be lost or misunderstood in translation, but "stew" is not something that is easily mistaken. It could be less about the "stew" and more about a detail to pinpoint who is watching over them.

The next day, I received this email:

"Wanted to let you know that, without telling him we had a pet-psychic session, Dave asked his dad if his grandpa or any other male family member was known for making stew of any kind. Dave's dad was so thrown off and immediately asked, 'How would you ever know that? Why are you asking that?' Turns out that it was, indeed, his grandpa. He used to make this squirrel stew that was a local hit. He even sold it at a local bar. He also told us he was a crazy animal lover and used to always bring home neighborhood strays as a kid (something we never knew, either). Needless to say, we all had chills."

Heaven is wonderful place, full of love and mysteries. The animals do not feel lonely in Heaven. They do not miss us like we miss them. They can be with us, visit us, and live in a past memory, just as if it's the present time. Whenever you feel sad and distant from your loved ones in Heaven, call to them. Talk with them, and look for signs of their presence. They are trying to let you know that they love you, that they are OK, and that they are watching over you. Trust in those subtle feelings that you are not alone.

# The Ghost Dog

When I was 22 years old, I lived in a classic colonial house built in the 1800s. It sat down a long dirt driveway, surrounded by woods of maples and old Connecticut stone walls. On our third day living there, it took my boyfriend, Evan, and me half a day to transport two extremely heavy stone lions from the old, abandoned barn on the property to the front of the house.

After much back-breaking effort and sweat, we sat on the porch drinking wine, with our wolf-hybrid, Maia, running in and out of the pond with a stick, our Aussie, Stormy, at my feet, and our two cats, Joey and Makia, looking for chipmunks on the stone wall.

"They are a little eerie-looking," Evan commented, staring at the lions.

I surveyed them. They were the classic, regal lions you would see in paintings or on the steps of mansions. I was proud of our find and smiled. "They look like they should be guarding a castle or another dimension," I responded. "I like them."

Evan shrugged, pouring himself another glass of red wine. I could tell his mind was making up stories. "You read too much Stephen King," I said.

He leaned back in his chair and looked out toward the pond. It had started to drizzle. Fall colored leaves, and rain created ripples on the pond. "Maybe so," he sighed. There was a sound of thunder in the distance. "Let's finish our puzzle," he said, getting up and walking into the house.

The noises started that night. The front storm door opened and slammed just when we were getting ready for bed. Evan and I were diligent about securing doors, protecting cats from coyotes at night. My wolf-hybrid loved to roam as soon as night fell. Evan and I looked at each other questioningly, and then it happened again. Maia barked and ran down the stairs, with Stormy in tow. The cats ran under the bed. We heard creak after creak; it sounded like Maia racing up the stairs, but it wasn't Maia — she was still downstairs. Evan and I stood at the top of the stairs, looking down, and Stormy and Maia looked back up at us as if saying, "Someone came in the door, right? We don't see anybody."

Then it happened again: the stairs creaked as if a large dog or multiple people were running up and down them.

I grabbed Evan's sleeve, with my heart beating strong. "OMG! We live in a haunted house."

Stormy, only six months old, growled.

"Just ignore it," said Evan.

"I have the chills all over, and the hair is standing up on my arms. How can I just ignore this?"

And then the house fell dead quiet — an eerie quiet that you never hear with four animals and in a house built in the 1800s. The windows didn't rattle, even though it was storming outside. "How could it get so quiet so fast?"

I was no stranger to haunted houses or seeing ghosts, for that matter. I grew up in a neighborhood where my friends' families had lived in homes for hundreds of years. I had slept in many houses occupied by spirits. I knew the feeling of a benevolent spirit as opposed to a malevolent spirit. This one was not malevolent, but it didn't feel human, either.

I fell asleep pretty quickly. Evan woke me up in the middle of the night, whispering in my ear, "Tomorrow we bring those lions back to the barn."

I wouldn't let him. I loved them too much, and he couldn't move them without me.

A few days later, I was washing dishes in the kitchen, and I heard scratching on the basement door. I thought I had accidently left Maia down there from when I was doing laundry. I opened up the door. No one was there. I called Maia, expecting to see her come from the basement, but she turned the corner from the living room. "What?" I questioned, and then I saw it: the door was all scratched up from the inside, with deep claw marks in the door. I became overwhelmed with sadness, and my heart was pained. "Jerk," I said to the memory of whoever was so cruel. Someone had locked a dog down there. It was a creepy basement — stuffy, dark, and unfinished, with dirt and rocks as walls. Our ghost must be a dog. "I am sorry," I said to the air, hoping he was still there.

That night I was woken up by a muzzle poking me in the face. I thought it was Maia, but when I opened my eyes, there stood a spirit, a tall Irish Wolfhound with gorgeous amber eyes. He looked at me and asked, "Can I stay here?"

I answered, "You are welcome to stay here. We love you. But know there is a better place for you — Heaven, with light and love. Feel the love, and you will be there." He reached his head toward me, and, all of a sudden, a bright light surrounded him, and he disappeared in a flash.

"Turn off the light!" Evan mumbled, half asleep, putting a pillow over his head. There was no light on. That light was from another dimension.

Our spirit Irish Wolfhound often came back to tease our guests by pushing the front door open or running up and down the stairs, but he was lighter now. I often saw him running alongside Maia in the yard, carrying his own stick or lying at the foot of our porch between the two lions.

# The Other Side of Air

Alfred was a 16-year-old Jack Russell Terrier. He died in April of 2017. In March, at the end of his life, his person asked me to speak with him. She wrote, "Al is very old. I don't have your gift, but I am sensitive to my critters. Al is giving me mixed signals. I want to know how he is feeling in his advanced age."

During our session, Al said, "I am feeling a little more distant lately. There seems to be more sunshine on the other side of air. It's a soft feeling. Dogs are running there. Some small Jack Russells like me and a big one, too. The big one rolls in the tall grass. He is smiling. I also see a man who says he will take me walking. He is throwing a stick.

"Sometimes I feel happy inside of myself. My mom is sweet and tender to me. She has been feeding me really well. I have times where I am happy in my legs. But when I am feeling sick, I feel confused about what time of day it is. I love my life, but I am spending more time in the sunshine on the other side of air. It is getting close to that time when I will cross the bridge to the other dogs. That rainbow bridge is really fun looking. I would love to see grass. I am not scared, because there is love in that world. I know you can feel your mom hugging you there, because sometimes when I am in that world, I have mom hugs and dad smiles. It's a peaceful place.

"When I am awake, I get anxious, and my legs start to get anxious, too. I think I need to eat a lot of chicken pieces and lick some ice cream. That would be great. Maybe I could eat a hamburger."

The reason why Al's person was sensing mixed signals is because the veil between dimensions started to dissolve. When Al would awake from his dreams or from visiting the afterlife, he would seem renewed, but as he stayed awake, he became more aware of his pain and his decline in health.

Al died peacefully a few weeks after our first conversation. A week after his passing, I connected with him again. He said, "Tell my mom that Heaven is really beautiful. I can run fast again, leaping over the couch in our living room and spinning around. My mom's dad is here. He met me over the bridge, took me in his arms, wrapped me in a blanket, stroked me like my mom does, and said, 'You are home, Al. You are not sick anymore.' Just then, full of energy, I got up and ran outside and all around the grass. My breathing is really easy now. My mom's mom is here, too. She kisses me, makes sure I eat well, and brings me water. We have been on beach walks! I want to tell my mom that I am relieved that I am not in that body anymore. It was hard dying. Now I am all my spirit and all the love my family has for me. I am still with her. I visit all the time. I sit on the couch with her and snuggle up beside her. I prance into the kitchen with her, and sometimes I sit on the passenger seat of the car. I love it here. I had the best life with my mom. I still feel her here. I don't feel I am missing her, because we are all one."

Often it is we who struggle when our loved ones pass over, but they have transitioned to a world filled with love. Our loved ones will visit us in spirit and place a memory into our minds while wrapping their spirit around us. Oftentimes, that memory comes with intense emotion. One may feel love, laughter, joy, or sorrow. The mind may have a hard time understanding it and fall into a sense of longing. Take a moment to be present when you are overcome. Speak out to your loved ones, and then notice how you feel. You just may feel a comforting love surround you — a visit from what Al calls "the other side of air."

# A Reincarnation Story

Every now and then, I get down. When I am in a state of self-pity or ruminating about trauma, I lift myself up by looking at the miracles in life. These miracles are not only proof of a web of energy that fuels us and loves us, but they are proof that there are loved ones in our lives who are "meant" to be with us. This story is just that.

In April 2018, I had a session with a woman named Mary, who had a feeling that her cat, Jack, was going to reincarnate back to her. Jack had died three weeks earlier at the age of 14.5. Mary wanted to see if I could talk to him in spirit and find out more information. Often, animals do return to us in another body. Although my work has found hundreds of reincarnated souls, I never guarantee that I will be able to find them. I explained to Mary that reincarnation is extremely complex. Sometimes the animals give us concrete descriptions of when and where they will be found. Other times, they offer little clues about their return that send people on treasure hunts that can last for months and possibly years.

Jack said he wanted to come back in the fall of 2018 and that he would be the same color as he was in his past life but with more white and zigzag orange. He also mentioned a friend of Mary's.

On October 3rd, we had another session to check in with Jack. He told me he was in body. He said he was imagining sleeping in Mary's arms. He said he was a kitten who was no longer with his mother at a shelter "that has a no-return policy," which I felt was a county shelter because, at those, you don't have to bring the animals back if they are not working out. He said that he "is farther away, in a place that has a night-time feel." Mary volunteered at a shelter 20 miles east of her. I felt like Jack was saying that he was toward the west (sunset) and that he was at a shelter farther away than the shelter Mary volunteered at. Mary mentioned that the "friend" we spoke of last time told her about kittens to the west of her. I didn't feel Jack was one of those kittens, but I did feel this was a sign Jack is back in a body. Jack said, "There is kindness, the sound of water dripping, and the sound of a broom where I am." He told us, "I am not eating good food. I have a bellyache. But I am rambunctious and happy."

Mary got off the phone with me thankful, but a little upset. How was she going to find him with those descriptions? Really?! I assured her that, if it was meant to be, it would all make sense in time. The next day, Mary took the day off to look for him at shelters west of her.

I received this email from Mary a few days later:

"Hi Laura: Found him! His instructions described the Loudoun County Animal Shelter near Leesburg, Virginia. It was the fourth shelter I visited last Thursday, and I was getting upset that I had not found him yet. The dripping was a ceiling-mounted A/C unit and/or the sink. There were brooms in the corner. He also kind of 'burped,' like his belly was bothering him. As I was holding him close to my face, I asked him, "Is this really you, Jack?" and he head-butted my chin! I was so happy and trying not to cry with Joy. 'Cracker Jack' is now home. I cannot thank you enough! And now, he is 'sleeping in my arms' for real!

"Warm regards, Mary."

# Riding the Wind Back to Life: A Reincarnation Story

As soon as I heard my client's voice on the phone, I knew she was still in pain. She sounded shaky and withdrawn. "Eight months ago, my seven-year-old dog died in his sleep. I can't relax or stop thinking about why he died. I feel guilty because I don't know what happened."

Her dog, Little Danny, had been staying with in-laws when he died, and, although she did not suspect any foul play or secrecy, she was confused about what caused a seemingly perfectly healthy dog to die in his sleep.

In my work, I hear stories like this all the time. Usually, in the photographs of the pets that people send me, I can see signs of illness. Crinkled brows of headaches, gritting teeth, or moping, painful smiles. But that was not the case with Little Danny's photo. He was a small, white pit bull with beautiful dalmatian-like spots, gleaming vibrant eyes, and a smile that said, "I am one of those happy pit bulls that kids can roll all over."

Animals don't like to see their people suffering, so they often talk about how wonderful dying is and who met them. Danny says, "When I died, I felt a lifting up into graceful play, not a slamming body play. I died in my sleep chasing a rabbit into the bushes. A bird jumped out, and then I leapt for it and flew. Your dad met me. He taught me 'shake' and loves to see my tail wag. We went to the ocean together."

I asked him if he knew what had caused his death. Danny answered, "I got really tired inside, like an anesthesia feeling. I had a pushing and pulling feeling inside, not a burning. I felt like I'd taken too much sleep medicine. Do you know that medicine?" This made it sound to me like Danny had a tumor that had bled out. This can make them exhausted until they pass away.

Danny continued, "I am learning how to squeak toys and run with the squeaky toys. *Shhhh*. I have a secret. I found a body for me, and I am close to my mom and dad. I am home, at a place with trees and a field. I am back." I asked if I understood him correctly. "Are you reincarnated and in body now?" This always makes me a little nervous, because then, the search starts.

Danny answered, "Yes. *Shhh*. Mommy has to figure it out herself. I can snuggle up close with her. You know that my mom is looking at me now and smiling, because she sees me." I read this to Danny's person, and she gasped. The day before, she'd gotten a Poodle puppy. He has been running around with a squeaky toy and lies upside down with his head hanging off the bed. Just that morning, she had been saying how much the new dog reminded her of Danny and how he sits just like Danny.

"Are you the new Poodle puppy, Remy?" I ask Danny.

"I am in Remy." He says joyfully, "I am happy to be home. Now I can live a long life. There is magic in Heaven. Grandpa said, 'This is a sad story that needs to turn upside down. Then he kissed me and sent me home.' He said, 'It's easy to ride the wind back home when you want to. It's time. You're a gift for your mommy and daddy." Our deceased friends and family members are always helping us from the other side.

Danny added, "Don't be scared to die, mom, because when you die, you become an even more beautiful self. Then you become one with everything, and that oneness helps guide you home."

# Chapter 6

# WILDLIFE

# The Hawk and the Mourning Dove — February 2010

There have been times in my life when I have asked for advice and I have heard, "Follow your heart" as the reply. To become proficient in my work, I have tried to dissect and study every acute feeling within me. I question what is coming from the heart and what is coming from the mind. I have tried to let go of the mind, follow my intuition, and see beauty in the not-so-distant future. Every day I tell animals, "The smartest animals in the world are conscious of their behaviors. If you want to be one of the most brilliant animals in the world, you have to know what you are doing at every moment and why."

I am at a crossroads in my life. The odds that are at stake are great. I want to take a chance and travel one way, but branches have been falling in front of me. The other path is clearer. There is a possibility that the branches are a test and will be removed if I keep walking, but there is also the possibility that the falling branches are warnings, and, if I don't change direction quickly, larger limbs will fall, and I could become injured. I am aware that both paths will reveal lessons needed to learn, magic, and beauty, but one of these paths could reveal unnecessary hardships that could be avoided.

Yesterday, a Red-shouldered Hawk landed with a mourning dove in his talons just outside my window while I was working. When I went outside to get a better look, he just sat on the dove and stared at me. I told him my property was a no-kill zone. He didn't move. The dove was frozen beneath him. I went to get my camera. When I came back out, the hawk sharply gazed at me and hopped off the dove to the ground. To my surprise the dove was still alive! She fluttered, disoriented, and then flew fast and graceful across the street, dropping feathers in her wake. The hawk took flight and followed her trail.

For some reason, I now turn to them for advice. How should I decide which path to travel?

Mourning Dove says, "When the hawk held me down, I heard him wonder, 'If I kill her, will I be punished? Death should not happen in the air or on the land inhabited by the one who can speak to the animals if that is her wish.' He did not kill me. He became conscious and alert to the rhythms of divine judgment. Yesterday, I wanted to feed on the seed you leave for us beneath the purple flowers, but something inside of me told me not to go there. I ignored the feeling, because I have always felt safe on your territory. It was my fault I came upon danger. I was warned. I should have stopped, thought, and gone elsewhere. When I am troubled by which way to go, I look up, and then I look within. I feel a gentle stream of energy that will direct my direction of travel. That is the way I always try to choose. If you feel heaviness when you walk, meditate, find that gentle stream of energy, and then change direction."

The hawk says, "You have told me before that I am not allowed to hunt on your land. I felt a strong sense I should not go for the dove, but she was tempting in her plumpness. I thought I could keep it a secret from you. When I landed with her in my talons, it was your eyes that met me first. I immediately saw your sadness and I felt like I had dishonored you. I still wanted the dove, but when you wanted to capture the memory on camera, I realized I did not want that moment to be saved. I let her go so you would see I am capable of hearing you. I flew after her because that is where I was being pulled. I saw her huddled in the bushes, and I left her there because I knew if I went after my temptations, somehow you would know she had been killed. My advice to you is to follow your heart's path on territory that you know will not hurt yourself or someone else. It is not bad for me to hunt Mourning Doves. I just needed to respect my inner knowing and your sacred territory."

# A June 2008 Morning

This morning, as I lay in bed after one push of the snooze button, the ravens outside begin to squawk incessantly. I know this sound well. They are mobbing a Red-tailed Hawk. I listen more closely. There is a distant distress call of the hawk's mate. I breathe in and breathe out, and the incessant squawking continues. I lift myself up from a small space in the middle of my king-size bed, carefully trying not to disturb my five sleeping companions (my two dogs and three cats) with my clumsy dawn movements. I squint my eyes and go to the east-facing bedroom window. "Where are the ravens?" I ask myself. I see them in the distance, perched on an ancient oak. I, by no means, have a hawk's eye. I perceive in the field what I think is a downed raven. I look for a hawk but don't truly see one. I see the raven's deep-black wing flapping against the green dewy grass. I wonder, "Do I go out there and interfere with nature? Do I rescue the raven? Take it to Wildlife Rescue to see if it can survive? Should I chase a hawk away?"

I believe we are all a part of nature and that there is no solid answer to this question. If we listen to our intuition in the present, we will know exactly what to do. So, I pull on my

Ugg boots, grab an old towel, and jog out to the field, leaving my animals bewildered and snoozing on the bed.

When I get to the scene, the Red-tailed Hawk is on the ground eating the raven. The hawk is placid and allows me to approach. I stand twenty feet from him and watch. The raven's spirit is no longer suffering, but his companions are relentless. They perch above, squawk, and dive at the hawk. They are mourning their friend. Standing in the midst of it all, I wonder, "When do the ravens accept that there has been a death and that there is no more that they can do? Is their behavior a ritual to honor the killed raven? Is it to prove something to the Red-tail?"

The Red-tail's mate flies above and calls out. She, too, is hungry. The male Red-tail looks up decisively and flies to a tree carrying the raven and then to the branch of another tree closer to my house. I follow him, as do a large flock of ravens. The hawk allows me to be ten feet away from him. He is peaceful. Many ravens join him in the branches of the oak tree. He waits patiently and preens a feather from his breast. It sticks to a branch and then floats into my hand. We talk about giving thanks, companions, and praying. We talk about what it is like to be hit by numerous ravens while in flight. I want to talk to the ravens about acceptance, but they are too upset. I admire both the hawk and the ravens. I admire the hawk for his calmness, patience, and confidence around the unwavering chaos, and I admire the ravens for their loyalty and perseverance. I spend some time with them all just being present, and then I say goodbye and walk away. As my back turns, the squawking seems a bit quieter. As I approach my home, the Mourning Doves' coo-cooing becomes the predominant noise. The Native

195

Americans believe the Mourning Dove's call is a sign, "to mourn the past and to be open to the promise of the future."

I am back in my bedroom now writing this. Out the north window, I can hear the Mourning Doves cooing and, out the east window, the ravens are still squawking. I begin to reflect, "For how long do we mourn the past?"

# The Call of the Wild, in Civilization

A few years ago, just before nightfall, I accompanied my friend to a car-dealership event attended by about 100 people. Cartoon-character balloons larger than buildings bobbed in the near distance, and bright, flickering fluorescent lights illuminated deals of the year. The crowd mingled quietly. Toddlers and young children were silhouetted against their parents, who, oddly, seemed to bob like the enormous balloons.

My date was there to make an appearance and to see an old friend. I selfishly went to observe and to talk to the leopard, whose company was hired to bring him for entertainment.

At the time I arrived, the crowd was not showing much interest in the spotted leopard (*Panthera pardus*). I watched before I approached. He had three handlers who took turns holding his chained leash inside a cage.

I immediately noticed that the leopard, if he wanted to, could easily scale the 15-foot fencing and get away. I concluded that the cage was more to keep the human spectators away. The handlers asked him to "sit," "stay," "stand on box," and "beg." Even I, a former animal trainer, thought, *How humiliating.*

I was taught by my teachers long ago not to feel sorry for animals in front of them. They said that doing so could worsen their situation, and that, we, as animal advocates, should give the animals confidence and power to transcend their suffering. I believe this, but I have also come to see that acknowledging another's suffering gives them a sense of peace and, from there, they can build strength to overcome.

The leopard was long, lean, and graceful. He walked with complete and utter awareness. When he was not putting on a show, he watched the crowd with an acute eye. *What is he watching?* I thought. He stood up and sniffed, crouched down, peered into the crowd, and then lay down again, still watching. I scrutinized the crowd, too, thinking, *What is he so intent on?* Then I noticed.

He was watching the children. Instinctually, feeling me watching him, he turned to me. "I can hear you in my head," I whispered.

He was not surprised; with odd domestication, he said, "Will you tell my woman trainer the transport cage is slippery? She'll fix it better than the others." He then huffed twice and continued scanning the children.

I spoke to the handlers. I wanted to be annoyed by them for being a part of his captivity, but they were open to my communications and generous with information. They spoke of working with exotics to educate the public. They said, "Most people think all big cats are lions." I believed them. Their sense of mission was compelling, and their training methods were clearly humane.

But something still didn't sit right with me. I lived with Maia, my late wolf-dog, who was stuck between two very different worlds: domestic life and her wild instincts. Maia and the leopard were similar. Both of them instinctually surveyed the perimeter of their environment and noticed every sound, smell, and movement. It would take just a moment for him to leap, slip the chain from the distracted handler's hand, scale the enclosure, and devour a child a few feet away. He had incredible impulse control.

"Thank you for restraining yourself," I said to the leopard.

"You noticed? It's hard," he answered.

"Yes," I replied. I took a breath and asked, "What is life like for you?"

The leopard stretched himself closer to me, but he still kept his eye on the crowd. "Something is missing. I need to run faster and farther. My muscles are weak. I should hunt and pick my own food, but they give me food that tastes dull. My body is not satisfied."

"How do you feel about your training?" I asked, trying to stay positive about something he had accomplished.

"It keeps me focused and alert. The people are kind. I feel trapped," he answered.

I got closer to the cage and bent down beside him. Our eyes were less than a foot apart. "I am sorry. There are people who don't believe in the way you're being made to live, and they fight to keep animals in the wild or in more natural environments. These people are your species' voice, and they will make life better for others like you. I promise. You are beautiful. Thank you for being the best you can be in your situation. It helps others like you, and it helps people learn about your species."

He blinked his eyes and then stared off into the distance, past the people, the balloons, the parking lot, and off into an agricultural field. "Humans who know how we feel?" he questioned.

"Yes," I answered. "What would you like to tell the ones who don't know?" I asked.

"Don't take us from the wild. We know what we are missing. Let us smell the soil and our prey in the wind. Let us lay our bodies on the earth. So many of your noises hurt us. If you trap us, let us hear the sound of the trees or the rush of the rivers."

Just as he spoke, a car drove by and honked its horn. For a moment, the leopard's eyes dulled, and his face acutely quivered. *Clearly, he has been traumatized*, I thought.

It took all my strength to hold back my pity and my tears. With an open heart, I showed him only honor for the exquisite being he is. He raised his head with dignity and caught the sight of a hawk flying over the fields. We both let out a soft breath and watched the hawk rise with the wind.

# My Friend the Rat

Night had just fallen. My two Chihuahua mixes, Felix and Easter, my Poodle, Luca, and my white German Shepherd, Hudson, stood with their chins raised, staring up into the branches of the ash tree in our backyard, their front legs tapping and bouncing, their tails straight out behind them.

I thought nothing of it.

Then a small, dark figure dropped from the tree and smacked hard against the metal cover of the firepit. The dogs instantly went into pursuit. The breath ran out of me. *Did they catch him?*

I sprang into action. "Leave it! No Kill Zone," I said, with my voice just louder than a whisper, intensifying my energy and my body language toward one dog in prey drive and then to another.

The dogs froze; their eyes pierced the darkness toward my feet. There was the little animal, moving as I moved, safely cushioning himself to the arch of my left foot.

"Into the house," I ordered, pointing at the back door. One by one, the dogs ran inside.

*Where did he go?* I wondered.

My eyes caught him under the glass lawn table, hiding behind the leg of a chair, his little eyes peering out at me and catching the light from the kitchen window.

*Please do not be hurt*, I whispered inwardly, filling my heart with love and sending him compassion.

"Are you alright, little guy?"

To my amazement, the little rat blinked his eyes, reached his tiny paws upward, stretching his body up the chair leg. Then, with a curiosity equal to mine, he climbed up to the top of the chair and came to rest twelve inches from my face.

"I am out of breath," he shared. His small torso rapidly expanded in and out. His head was awkwardly tilted to the side, and one eye appeared to bulge.

Tears filled my eyes. I thought, *He must be in pain.* I quivered.

"Did the dogs get you?" I asked.

"No, you kept me safe. I hit my head when I fell."

"How did you know that I would keep you safe?" I questioned.

"I am the rat," he replied. "The one you have been talking to. I left your attic and stopped pooping on your outdoor parrot cage because it's unsanitary. I moved my family next door when you told me you were getting a cat. I have done everything you have asked because you have taken the time to explain to me what you need and why. In return, you don't trap me or poison me, and I get to drink water out of your fountain and eat food that the parrot drops on the ground. We live harmoniously."

"Thank you for listening to me."

"Is it safe to go home now?" he asked, blinking his eyes tiredly.

"Yes," I told him. "It is safe to go home."

And with that, my friend the rat scurried down the chair, across the yard, and up the bamboo adjacent to the ash tree, leaving me with the sense of wonder of a child.

# Captive Orca Whale

* This article was written in 2010. In January of 2017, Tilikum died. Seaworld claims he died of a bacterial pneumonia. Blackfish co-writer Tim Zimmermann wrote for *National Geographic,* "His life has changed how we view SeaWorld and the marine-park industry, and changed our moral calculus regarding the confinement and display of intelligent, free-ranging species."

* As of August 29, 2019, the Whale and Dolphin Conservation states that at least 166 Orcas have been taken into captivity from the wild since 1961. Presently, 60 Orcas are held in captivity. 29 have been captured in the wild and 33 were born in captivity. Since 2002, at least 19 Orcas have been taken from the wild into captivity.

On February 24, 2010, an Orca Whale named Tilikum killed Dawn Brancheau, his trainer of 16 years at SeaWorld Orlando. Tilikum is a large adult male. He was captured in the waters of Iceland at the age of two, 30 years ago. In 1991 and 1999, he was involved in the death of two other people. Dawn and Tilikum had just finished what seemed to be a very good public session. Tilikum had done spins for her, and she had just petted and hugged him. Witnesses said that Tilikum "looked like he was playing" and then "just took off really fast, came back around, bobbed up in the water, and grabbed her. He was thrashing her around pretty good." SeaWorld Orlando says they are going to keep Tilikum active in their show program. Animal activists have many arguments about the inhumanity of keeping Orcas in captivity. For one, in the wild, they swim all day and night. It is unnatural for them to be in such small concrete enclosures unable to forage for food, dive deep, mate, or listen to the natural sounds of the ocean. Tilikum had been witnessed being bullied by other whales. In the wild, he would be able to swim away from conflict. In the wild, they live in stable groups with very little violence. Family units stay together for life and have their own language. In captivity, Orcas may not even know how to communicate with each other. Their family structure is constantly changing as they are moving to different facilities. Many argue that captivity creates a level of inner stress that can cause Tilikum to act in dangerous, unpredictable ways

I cannot talk to Tilikum without SeaWorld Orlando's permission, but I can talk to another, anonymous, captured Orca and tell them what happened and ask them what their thoughts are.

Anonymous Male Orca Whale: "I know what that whale did. Everyone has been talking about it, and they have been staying farther away from our enclosure than normal. People who did not fear us fear us now. Sometimes we do not get fed enough. We have pains in our stomachs because we do not get the right kind of fish. They don't feed us the variety that we would get in the wild, and so our stomachs are always feeling uncomfortable. Tilikum is like many others. We do tricks for them, and we have a sense that they are our guardians; we care for them to some degree, but we dislike their species. Those of us that have lived in the wild know that how we live now is torture. The water burns our skin, the light damages our thoughts and our brains, the food does not nourish, and our muscles feel weak because we cannot work them like we would in the wild.

"The sounds in the waters here are clanking. They are not natural. We long for the sounds that we heard in the wild waters. The temperature of the water is wrong. It makes us feel abnormal and incautious. I know Tilikum suffers like we all do. Our brains and body do not work as they should. We want to survive. We see people only as our means to nourishment. I can only speculate, but I would imagine that they were not feeding Tilikum a well-balanced diet. His stomach probably ached, and his eyes hurt from the water and the light. His trainer may not have given him the right number of fish for a trick, or she may have fed him smaller ones. They don't understand that they are not feeding us enough of what we would eat in the wild. We are not healthy. This is a miserable life for us.

"They keep us captured for reasons we do not understand. We should not be living in their environment. They should set us free."

# Talks with Cecil the Lion

Some of you may remember Cecil the lion from Hwange National Park in Matabeleland North, Zimbabwe. At 13 years old, he was wounded by an arrow shot by a trophy hunter. This hunter happened to be an American. The arrow did not kill Cecil right away. He was tracked through the night and then shot and killed by another arrow 10 to 12 hours later. His body was then skinned, and his head removed. It was an illegal hunt. People around the world mourned for Cecil and other wild animals like him.

On August 1, 2015, I contacted Cecil in Heaven and asked him about his experience. This is what he said:

"For many hours, my soul was exhausted. I tried to make sense of suffering, pain, the fight to live, and how to defend my pride. I had thoughts that I did not know that I had inside of me. I had thoughts of being weak, being scared and fearful, and being without my life. I realized that death was coming, and I felt strangely depressed. I didn't know I was able to have emotions like that. I wonder if this is how my prey has felt.

"Being hunted by humans seemed strange and out of nature. When they shot me, I felt the pain come slowly. I crossed a river of great darkness. I crossed a river of great sickness. These men are sick men.

"They think that, if they kill us, they control the nature and the energy that run through us, but they do not understand the true nature of energy.

"When they kill us, they are poisoning the field of energy that runs through all things. I have seen your cities and have seen inside your homes, and I fear for you. I fear now for my lands because the earth is ill. There are few people fighting for its ability to continue breathing."

In September 2015, I asked, "What is your Heaven like?"

Cecil said, "I am in the kingdom of the divine love. I am at the center of the circle of love. There is no fear where I am now. I am big and bold and powerful, and I am the protector of all. I watch over the people who fight for me. I watch over the organizations that write about and protect me. I am their hero and their noble light source. I am energized by the members of the human race who are touched by our plight. I am love. I give love, and I receive love. I want all to know that there is no more pain in my soul. I am honor. Thank you all for caring so deeply about me and others like me. Put your swords in your pocket, and arm yourself with words and action to make changes. Hear me roar when you are closed to change. I am your companion and your friend. I am free. There is only love within me now. The future will be kind. The future will be back to nature."

# Lessons from the Little Bird

I was at a meditation workshop. It was after the morning meditation and right before the lecture that I went back to my room for breakfast. A small gray bird the size of a sparrow flew in the door and perched on the ceiling fan. I spoke to him and told him the way out. He listened and flew in the direction of the door but too high. Panicked, he flew frantically trying to free himself, bouncing himself off the walls of the room until he tried to escape into the bathroom. I became a bit frustrated and worried, because all the mirrors and the glass door of the shower would be deadly to him, and time was closing in on having to be back for the lecture.

I found him perched above one of the mirrors above the sink. "Little guy, I am going to climb up there, put you in my hand, and take you outside. Now is the time to be brave. I promise you are safe."

He looked down at me, breathing heavily with wide eyes. "I am scared."

"Trust me," I responded. I was nervous because it was quite a climb up onto the vanity and a big reach to catch him. But, to my surprise, he waited for me. "OK, I am going to grab you and hold you softly in my hands. I promise I will take you outside."

He was skeptical. He sent me the feeling of "I am not that sure. I will see when your hand gets closer."

I grabbed him quickly and created a nest in my mind with my hands. He was startled at first and then peered out of the hole in my hands, soothed by my eyes. I felt him relax into my palm. "You are so brave," I told him. Coming from his little heart, I felt an overwhelming sense of gratitude and safety. He felt loved — there is no doubt.

I grabbed my iPhone to video him because he seemed so secure, and who doesn't want to catch that on camera? When I went for it and turned it on, he was unfazed by my movements. Once outside, I opened up my hand and expected that he would take flight immediately, but, to my delight, he just stood there looking at me. "You can fly, little guy. Your body is fine."

"I know," he said, looking at me with his adorable blinking eyes. "I just need to catch my breath." I smiled and laughed to myself. "You are such a brave guy," I said to him, lifting my thumb and stroking the side of his face and neck.

"I just need to catch my breath," he repeated very innocently.

He wasn't even breathing that heavily. I didn't want to rush my new friend, but it was getting close to the start of the lecture.

"You can totally fly," I encouraged him.

"I just need to catch my breath," he repeated, standing and calming himself in my palm.

"You are such a good boy." My heart filled with immense love for all the little creatures of this Universe. I feel it a great honor to be able to connect with them the way I do.

"I am?" he responded.

"Yes, you are." I took a step back, thinking I would perch him on a chair, and, with that movement, he set flight into the trees.

What did I learn? It's important to spend time with the divine essence inside of us that connects us to all things. Within that space, we radiate a greater love, a frequency the natural environment and the creatures of this Earth already live by. It's important to spend time with a community of people who are striving to become more conscious, healthier, and happier. Once you plug in to that, it doesn't take long to experience miracles. So, take the time to breathe, and see how life unfolds.

# Captive Grizzly

We were at an animal actors ranch, filming for a sizzle reel. The people were skeptics at first, but quickly became believers when the young mountain lion told me some of their secrets. When we were about to leave, I overheard the head trainer and the owner whispering, "Should we tell her?"

Turns out they had an issue on a movie set where their grizzly bear had escaped. After the incident, she became aggressive toward the head trainer. At the sight of him, she would pace and bang on her cage, making it impossible for him to handle her. My film crew was allowed to film only her cage in the compound. My heart blew up with shock, anger, and sadness over how the animals lived: cages smaller than 12 × 24, domestic cats in with monkeys. Jaguars, Siberian tigers, and the grizzlies housed shockingly close to one another. *So unnatural for predators of this kind to be so close — and shouldn't the grizzly be hibernating now?* I thought. I saw the behavior immediately — the fear in the grizzly's wide eyes, pacing, banging, and huffing. *She could kill him or anyone that reminded her of him,* I thought. He left the scene. I turned my body to the side, looked at her, and then looked away and approached the cage. She felt safe with me, approached me, and put her paw through the chain-link. I could feel the roughness of her pad on my fingertips. Her tongue stroked the back of my hand. I was in awe of her beauty. I had treasured the find of black bear fur off of trees in the woods, but here I could stroke the fur on her body and feel that she had loved humans' touch for a long time.

"My back (kidneys) and stomach hurts," she complained. Turns out they trained her with coffee nips and cheese doodles.

"He chased me," she explained about the trainer and the incident.

"He was trying to catch you so that you'd be safe," I told her.

"He was trying to attack me." She showed me images of him being firm with her, with his hands outstretched above his head and a forceful run toward her with a face growling.

"They don't know anything about bear body language. He used signs of aggression and didn't know it," I told her and then went into detail out loud so that her handlers could learn.

She sniffed the air and started to huff, preparing herself for a fight. She smelled him coming closer. I explained to her that she had PTSD and that she needed to raise her consciousness and realize that he loved her and was trying to help her. The trainer was able to get much closer to her, but I felt that her working on a set was putting others in danger. I wanted to yell at them, but I had learned to "meet everyone where they are," and yelling wouldn't have helped her. So, I explained that they needed to change her diet and learn more about her body language.

In the middle of the night, I was awoken by my front-door knocker knocking. Coincidentally, it is in the shape of a bear. No one was at the door, but the grizzly's presence was there with me — strongly. She told me she was suffering. Her back/kidneys were in pain. When she closed her eyes, she saw the trainer, a man she once loved, coming at her. I talked her through it. I prayed that I could heal her and take away her suffering. Her presence stayed with me throughout the night. When I awoke, I could not stand up. My back was in too much pain. After three days, unable to move, I went to the doctor's. It was my kidneys. If that was the price to pay for her peace, I would gladly take any animal's pain away. Now I know how to let it go. If I could only stop man's ignorance.

# Hanging with an Iguana Friend in Cancun

At a luxury resort in Cancun, Mexico, an iguana looked down at us with exquisite eyes from the pergola above my friends' hotel room. When I asked her why she was up so high, she answered, "I like the view of the ocean from up here. I can see where the other iguanas are. One of them picks on me." We told her to imagine both herself and that iguana at peace and to send him compassion. She thought about it, but did not respond.

I love watching reptiles eat. They eat with an unusual presence of mind, savoring each taste with delight. I asked her if she would like a treat. "I love strawberries," she replied. That was an easy request to fulfill from the breakfast buffet.

We named her "Joie" after Dr. Joe Dispenza. It seemed an obvious choice since we were attending his workshop. Joie became more and more comfortable with each feeding. One day we sat down with her to learn more about her. We quickly learned she was female when she asked us, "How many birthdays have you had?" She didn't mean how old we are. She wanted to know how many times we had given birth.

She got startled when someone walked behind her. I asked her why she was scared. She told us that she had seen other iguanas scooped up in nets and taken away. I explained to her that the resort staff was extremely compassionate toward animals so they were probably re-homing the other iguanas because of overpopulation. I explained the difference between staff uniforms and the guests' attire. She told us, "I have never known people to sing with their heart like you do." She was definitely talking about my friend, who sings beautifully throughout the day.

Joie then asked, "How many skies are there?" Because we were spending a lot of time meditating, we quickly assumed she meant dimensions to the Universe or states of mind, but Joie was being much more literal. She continued, "I like peaceful skies. I get scared of the storms. I have nowhere to hide."

I looked around. She had plenty of places to hide. Joie then showed me a wild storm. *She must be talking about hurricanes.* I explained to her that people at the resort love animals and that, during these storms, she should just run inside the hotel. The staff would be kind to her then. My friend, Marna, gave her directions on how to get into a nearby corridor that is contained, but still has lots of plants. It would be a safe place for her to take shelter during a hurricane and extremely close to where she was presently living. I told Joie to go explore the area in the middle of the night or early in the morning, so she would know exactly where to go. She liked that idea and found great comfort in it. I also told her we were leaving and that she could manifest strawberries by looking at people and thinking "strawberry" over and over, or, while looking at the "peaceful sky," imagining herself happily eating strawberries. Of course, she could manifest this, too. She manifested us.

We had this conversation as she feasted on strawberries, melons, and a banana. Afterwards, she stretched out on the grass and relaxed into her belly with her legs sprawled out. One did not need to be a pet psychic to see her gazing into our eyes with wonder. She is clearly fond of us and will miss us when we are gone. The feeling is mutual. Until we meet again, sweet Joie.

# Snake in the Temple

In 2008, at Lehigh University, I attended six days of teachings with the Dalai Lama. While in the auditorium, deep in meditation, I was approached in the psychic realms by three monks. They explained to me that, back home in Sri Lanka, they were having problems with an Indian python that had taken up residence in their temple. Although the snake was non-venomous, slow moving, and non-aggressive, its mere presence was frightening people away. I told them that I could help them. We planned to meet at lunch.

On the soft Pennsylvanian summer grass, under a maple tree, the four of us ate veggie sandwiches as I explained to the snake that she was scaring people and asked her if she would please consider moving her territory. She said, "I will not harm anyone. It's peaceful here. I like being special. They say prayers, have rituals, and hang flags for me. If I leave, I will miss them too much."

The three monks chuckled and explained that the rituals and prayers they are saying for her are actually prayers asking the spirits to move her from the temple.

I asked them, "Is there another place that is more suited for her to inhabit, where you can visit and honor her daily?"

They thought for a moment and conversed with each other in a language I did not understand. As if mirroring each other, their eyes squinted, they breathed, their hands traveled up to their chins and then back down to their laps, smoothing out their robes. One of them turned to me. His eyes looked honestly into mine, and then he replied, "If she moves out of the temple, down the steep embankment to the stone wall under the trees, before the river, she can live the rest of her life there. We will build her an altar and pray for her every day."

As I began to close my eyes to tell the snake, I noticed that all three monks had tears streaming down their cheeks. They nodded to me and then closed their eyes. I knew their intention was to match my telepathic frequency so that they could not only listen to my conversation with her but also learn to "speak snake."

I explained to her the monks' compromise and their promise. I sent her love and told her about the monks' tears. She thought for a moment; my heart expanded with a deep, welling sense of gratitude and love. Then a vivid image of her formed in our minds. I was shocked and in awe of her size and beauty. Her body was more than 10 feet long and wider than a large man's calf. She lifted her head off the ground, revealing dark streaks behind her brilliant eyes; her body was a beautiful sandy color with patches of darker brown. She answered, "As long as I can hear the recitations of their prayers for me, I will stay out of the temple." She lay her head back down on the ground and gracefully slithered out of the temple door, down the embankment, resting up against the stone wall.

In unison, the four of us returned to her our feelings of gratitude and love. Spilling from my heart, I said, "Thank you, sweet thing. You are truly a special snake."

I opened my eyes. The monks were beaming with gratitude.

Back home in California, I asked her, "Did the monks do as they promised?"

She answered, "As I stretch out on the top of the wall, people come closer to me than ever before. There is a beautiful altar with a jewel in the center. Flags hang above the path that leads from the temple to the wall. They come here morning, mid-day, and night to say prayers and leave offerings. They smile and talk to me as if I am one of their children. They love me more than I could have imagined. I am so thankful for them and for you. They have kept their sacred promise, and I have kept mine."

## Chapter 7

# DIARY OF A PET PSYCHIC

★ I wrote the next two articles after my local town was affected by the Montecito Mudslide Disaster. Montecito, California, was the first town I lived in when I moved from New York to California in my mid-twenties. I owned my first business there; it was a professional pet-sitting and dog-hiking business called "All Creatures Great and Small." I know every back road and trail in this town. I also know people who lost their lives in this disaster and many people and animals who decided to stay instead of evacuating, causing them to witness the tragic mudslide firsthand. This disaster came on the heels of the Thomas Fire, a fire that raged around my small town of Ojai, California, burning my horse's farm and many homes and farms of the people I love in 440 square miles. These two articles were written in a time of great mourning and gratitude.

# The Montecito
# Mudslide Disaster

I was surprised when my friend said that I was not as affected by the mudslide disaster as most of the Santa Barbara community. "You are more equipped to deal with it, because you speak to deceased people and animals for work," he told me. I wanted to argue with him and defend my intense pain and explain that, as a "psychic," my body and mind are continuously being flooded with the fear, exhaustion, intense guilt, shock, sorrow, and flashes of the destruction that everyone affected have been through.

*When I look into the survivors' eyes, I am them.*

But I know better than to argue this. I know that these waves of emotion and images do not just happen to "professional psychics." They can happen to any compassionate, empathetic individual.

My friend knows that I can ultimately navigate these feelings. He knows that it is in my beliefs that I find another reality that offers me comfort and a way out of my overwhelming suffering.

I choose to believe that being of service heals pain and helps others to recover. I believe that the love and energy put out by prayer and deep-hearted compassion give strength to others. This strength may feel as if it's coming from an invisible force within or from a greater being outside of ourselves.

From speaking with thousands of deceased beings, I have learned that *even though one dies a traumatic death, it does not mean that they suffered at the moment of their passing.*

Loved ones, ancestors, friends, and angels help us cross over and surround us in blissful serenity even before we die. On the other side of terror — or even threaded through it — angels are working in our favor. The proof of this is in subtle messages, like the slow, approaching awareness of the wind blowing or the sun coming out of the clouds. It might be that rainbow the day after the storm or memories of our deceased loved ones emerging gracefully, filling us with a softness or a smile. I believe in divine guidance, and there are no limits to it. Proof of this may be in important information or someone offering help coming at just the right time.

At first, when the shock of another disaster hits me, I am like many others fighting that feeling. Being in pain is honoring the dead and all that suffer. We must surrender to the pain, experience it, honor it, and then, with an acute eye and open heart, notice and be grateful for the little blessings that are around us. We have to let go of the debilitating pain. Our loved ones do not want us to suffer. I know this for a fact. They want us to believe in their presence and for us to seek out peace. Synchronicities, coincidences, and perfect timing are just them and the force of the Universe showing us that they exist and that we are worthy of happiness.

When trauma overwhelms me, I remember: Breathe, and be kind, grateful, forgiving, and reflective. Let go of resentments, honor the pain, and then be watchful and open to a different perspective. There are miracles happening all around us. It is up to us to be open to noticing them. When I do this, something of value always emerges for me to hold dear.

# How to Get Over
# the Trauma

Over the course of the last few months, the animals of our area and beyond have been asking me about the fires and the mudslide. A common theme is questions about being buried. Who, when, how, and what does that mean? They also ask me about all the helicopters in the sky. Reading my notes from these communications made me depressed. The animals of these regions have been so confused. They, too, have been wrapped up in the usual smells of fire and mud, the poor air quality, the sounds of helicopters and sirens, all the evacuations, and the complete despair of the people around them.

So instead of listing these sad communications here, I have asked my animals what their advice is for dealing with the trauma. My animals lived through evacuating my horse, Jubilee, from the fire as it took the ranch as well as evacuating from our own home. They have also been with me when I have spoken to people and animals that experienced the mudslide firsthand.

> Luca, my seven-year-old Poodle, says, "I spoke to a
> dog at a doggy daycare (in Santa Barbara, California)
> whose dog friend was buried in mud. He told me

his friend's spirit came to him in a dream. His friend said he was scared for only a moment when his house crumbled. He said the sky was filled with angels of all species. These angels guided the dead to Heaven."

Luca continued, "I have learned that, when something bad happens, there are always angels making it easy on your soul. I trust in that."

Easter, my four-year-old Chihuahua mix, says, "I say play with your animals, and you both will feel better. I do this all the time. Also, find a friend to hang out with so you don't feel so alone."

Felix, my six-year-old Chihuahua mix, says, "When I have memories of bad times, I force myself to think about all my friends who love me and all the fun things I do. Then the monsters in my head don't seem so suffocating."

Clyde, my four-year-old Flemish Giant rabbit, says, "I find going out in the yard to dig is the best way to deal with trauma. Some people are helping to find important things in the mud. I think that is awesome."

Ella, my five-year-old Snowshoe cat, says, "Talk with your animals about what happened so they understand it. When I am confused, I get more stressed. Before this home and mom, I peed around the house when I was stressed. Now I understand,

and I pee in the box. If your animals are being naughty, talk with them. They are probably just confused."

Seamora, my 26-year-old Blue and Gold Macaw, says, "I had to go to the Menagerie bird store during the fire evacuations. I was in awe at the amount of people who got strong and cared to help the birds. Pay attention to the strength inside of you and others. Be in awe of yourself."

Jubilee, my seven-year-old Warmblood/Appaloosa mare, says, "I fight when I go through trauma. I fight hard, but sometimes I fight too much, and that messes me up and makes my relationships difficult. I am working toward trusting others to help me." Jubilee was extremely naughty during the Thomas Fire evacuation. She refused to get into my trailer. She was rearing and striking while she stared, wild-eyed and huffing, toward the flames. This forced me to make two other trailer trips out of the valley with other animals, leaving her at a farm where the perimeter trees were burning and leaving me with the stress of not knowing if authorities would let me back into the area to try again. She eventually got onto another, bigger trailer with the help of many people risking their safety with not only the danger of the fire but also with her behavior. Since her farm burned down, I moved her to Oregon to live with a herd and to be with a trainer who gets her. Six months after the Thomas Fire, she had to evacuate her farm in Oregon because of another fire. Even though the fire was close and other horses were stressed as well, Jubilee took a deep breath, pulled herself together, and walked onto the first load of trailers to evacuate. I was so proud of her!

Hudson, my three-year-old white German Shepherd, says, "I think the best thing people can do when they are going through trauma is to help others. Many people suffer. It helps to be useful. Know yourself and your thoughts, and send love to the world around you. See beauty wherever you look. Life is all in your attitude. Be patient, and the best course of action will show itself. I am still working on this myself sometimes."

# Something to Believe In: A Fish Story

In 2009, I was at dinner with a friend of mine when she asked me when I started to believe in a Higher Power. I had to really think about this. Since the time that I could consciously remember things, I was able to see and sense spirits. My mom always talked about fairies and creatures from other realms, and my father also occasionally saw spirits, which brought great amusement at cocktail parties. My grandparents and other relatives were devout Catholics, but I am not sure I grew up believing in their "God."

When I was twelve years old, I was vacationing with a girlfriend of mine and her family in Sandestin, Florida. At the time, it was a very remote area on the Gulf of Mexico. It was the kind of place where crocodiles were seen as often as deer in the New York countryside. We had heard that the weekend before, there was a fishing derby, but very few fish were caught. My friend and I loved a challenge, so we dug up some worms, put them in a coffee can, and grabbed her dad's fishing poles. The two of us rode her bike down to the docks to see if we could catch some fish.

It was a typical spring Florida day, warm and humid. The docks were empty except for a few older yachtsmen fiddling with their rigging in a different section of the harbor. My friend and I sat and lay on the old wooden docks with our lines in the water for what seemed like a long time. A manatee came to check us out. As she examined us from deep in the water, we could see how docile and kind her eyes were. I also remember a school of little minnows circling around the docks. To this day, I can smell the salty seaweed tide and the flowers in the distance.

We were just talking nonsense when my friend said that she'd recently decided that she was an atheist. I asked her what that meant, and she explained that she did not believe in God or a Higher Power. I wondered if I shared the same beliefs. This friend and I had a lot in common. We both were a little eccentric. We both were popular, but didn't conform to the typical private-school/country-club attire or engage in normal teenage-girl gossip and drama. We both were athletic and loved to climb high trees. We had a bit of an obsession with chimpanzees, and both of us carried and used a pocket knife wherever we went.

I contemplated being an atheist. Just because I saw and sensed spirits and believed in fairies didn't mean I believed in a Higher Power or God Consciousness. I wondered what would convince me. I thought about testing God. I decided that, if I called out to God to show me fish and a fish jumped out of the water and flopped onto the deck by our feet, *then* I would be convinced there was a God. I said this to my friend, stood up, reached my hands up to the sky, looked up, and called out as if I were commanding God, "If there is a God, then show us fish!" Mind you that this was before I knew that God had a history of multiplying fish.

It happened so suddenly and with such energy that I literally peed in my shorts. As far as the eye could see, fish sprang from the water. The calm waters became ripple upon ripple. The sound of splash after splash is etched in my mind. I gasped when one fish flopped onto the deck, bounced twice, and fell back into the water.

My friend and I did not speak. We just grabbed the fishing rods, ran to her bike, and rode home. I don't recall ever talking with her about it. The power of it was too shocking to address. I don't remember if we could process it at that time. I do remember that bike ride home — the wind in my face as my friend pedaled, the strong smells of the sand and the jungle. I felt grounded and present.

The first time I told this story, I was in my thirties. My friend sat across the table from me and listened attentively. At the end, she sat back in her seat, looked at me with deep conviction, and then laughed. Her response was, "Laura, that doesn't prove there is a Higher Power. That just proves you can talk to fish."

What do you think? Was it a Higher Power, or did the fish find it amazing that a young girl could speak with them and decided to give her a show, or was it just a coincidence? Knowing what I know now, I feel the fish and a Higher Power got together so that two girls could believe.

# Grandma and Grandpa —
# It's a Choice to Be Like Them

My great-grandma Johnson was born in 1888. At 99 years old, with wavy red hair and costume jewelry, she felt joy hearing that she looked like she was in her 70s. She told stories of her family's covered wagon being held up and robbed by Native Americans in Minnesota. As a child, she was ordered to stay up all night shooing flies off her baby sister's corpse and later went on to bury her 44-year-old daughter, my father's mother, and then a son, too. In her 90s, Grandma Johnson traveled often with her other daughter from Studio City, California, by bus to Las Vegas to play the slots, where she was frequently lucky. She had no qualms about cheating me (a fifth-grader at the time) in a game of gin rummy, with cards literally up her sleeve.

She bragged that she'd never been sick a day in her life and died at 99 taking a nap from her very first headache. I remember vividly, as a four-year-old, meeting her in the hallway between bedrooms. She was wearing a robe and had a look on her face of complete astonishment. She told me she had a vision — not a dream — of a crystal world where she had met her daughter and found peace and love. At that moment, she reached into her robe pocket and gasped, bringing out a large, shining crystal in her palm for both of us to witness. She held it to her heart, smiled large, and breathed deep, tears streaming down her cheeks. Even as a young child, I knew something amazing had happened — a glass rock had appeared from something like a dream. She was psychic, too. Many years before it materialized, she predicted the house and farm where I would grow up. "If there is nothing you can do about it, there's no point in worrying," she would say time and time again when someone complained.

My maternal Grandpa Minervini was a Marine Captain in WWII at Guadalcanal. He was responsible for many men's lives. He told me that God, the memory of sailing, and the words of great poets all helped him through the trauma and that, each day, he knew which men would die. He could sense it in their faces when they awoke, and, despite his feelings, he would try to raise their spirits only to find some dead by nightfall. Long after the war, while we played outside, not one plane would fly overhead unidentified. Making it a game, he would throw me over his shoulders, like he had done many men in war, carrying me, laughing and kicking, to safety. He ran the biggest electric business in New York City, cured himself naturally of prostate cancer, became pen pals with Nelson Mandela, and loved a good shot of vodka.

Why is it that people like this can go through great trauma and still find the joys in life, while others fall into deep depression and are debilitated by memories of the past? From a very young age, I have studied this myself. Recently, I have been privy to some information that has conceptualized what I already have known. The secret is all in the heart and our connection to spirit. What we do wrong is struggle with emotions like despair, guilt, shame, and anger, holding them rotting in our gut, and trying to will them away.

What is best to do is breathe them up with passion to the heart and feel. Once at the heart, it can feel awesome; it can hurt like clenching, stabbing pain; it can feel like dead space or boredom. I personally have felt all of those. It doesn't matter. Just keep with it, and conjure up elevated emotions like joy and gratitude. Try watching baby animals, my Giant Flemish rabbit, Clyde, or people smiling. Once you feel slightly happy, a magnetic energy is created, lifting your vision to the top of your head and then out to spirit. When this happens, you are more at a place to transform your emotions, change your life, heal from incurable diseases, manifest want you want, or just be present for a moment without stress. It sounds so easy — like gazing at the stars or watching the formations of clouds. Why not?

It is a much more elaborate scientifically proven skill that Dr. Joe Dispenza teaches, but it's a process that many people do naturally. Some people are just wired from birth to believe in possibility, to believe in health, to know that this life is supposed to bring us joy and that order comes after chaos.

My Grandma and Grandpa believed in themselves and that it is a gift to be alive. They believed they were connected to something greater than themselves. They stimulated their minds, found joy in the present moment, and, no matter what life threw at them, they always believed in miracles.

Life is an accumulation of our thoughts and choices. Be aware, and love into the coming year.

# My Nature Is Very Much Canine

Growing up, I was an adrenaline junkie. I enjoyed the bucking horses, fell in love with boys who drove fast, and stayed awake into the night reading Stephen King. I was the girl in the horror movies that grabbed a knife to check out the closet while everyone screamed, "No, don't be stupid! Run!" From my teens to my 30s, I talked to spirits who were trapped, helping them cross over, sought out haunted houses, got in psychic trouble with Marines exploring different dimensions, specialized in rehabbing canine aggression, and surfed in waters way too big for me. I learned how to get injured and to stand up like nothing had happened. As an Italian New Yorker, I learned to speak my mind, be committed, and fight for what I believe in, no matter what the cost.

Unfortunately, I thought relationships were the same: thrilling, painful, worth it. I let some real nice men go because they were too adoring and too still. In most relationships, I would stick it out with the bad ones like riding a bucking horse, even though I'd end up sore. Then, I realized that my skin was way tougher than I ever wanted it to be and that I experienced things I didn't want to remember. One day, I just made a decision that I was not going to live with any type of abuse anymore. I want stillness, safety, purity, and love as the dominant emotions in my life. Don't get me wrong — I am not a victim. I have had an amazing life witnessing miracles and beauty, but I did put up with too much pain.

I thought about what I teach the dogs when they are in conflict and feeling overwhelmed. I teach them to look toward their people, retreat, and then go do something positive that builds their confidence and calms their mind. So that is what I started doing. If someone got worked up arguing with me and couldn't be open to hearing my side, I looked within and stated to them, "I have to go. I am getting too overwhelmed."

I was proud of myself. I had a newfound peace. I had more creative energy. My projects took on new dimensions. People who were unhealthy for me drifted away. I liked that I was able to leave situations where I was getting stressed rather than force myself to tame my anxiety in the moment. I realized on a deeper level how all those dogs I'd rehabbed felt when they changed. Their hearts felt safer, so they were more able to learn and grow.

But then a friend took great offense to this new method of mine. She told me that when I walked away, she felt I was ending the friendship for good, even though I stated that I would talk to her at a later date. She felt betrayed by me. This shocked me because I thought we both would calm down and revisit the matter later when we both could have clear communication. Now I have to ask myself, "Is it possible that I can ruin good relationships by walking away and taking space?"

That is definitely not my intention. What is an appropriate time to leave and come back, and whose responsibility is it to reach out? Does it even matter?"

With dogs, depending on their anxiety level, they may need breaks for a few seconds, hours, days — or even a week. My nature is very much canine. I am just going to state it here. I don't want to fight anymore. I am sorry if I have to leave. I still love you.

# Finding Joy in a World of Suffering

I used to feel so much suffering of others that I would spend a full day in bed each week, literally sleeping just to feel "normal." I once spoke to a bear actor whose kidneys were in so much pain that the next day my back went out, and I could not walk for three days. I have cried countless nights over clients' animals dying of cancer, bunnies getting beauty products poured in their eyes, or people I know dying.

On my days off, I stayed in the woods avoiding people so that I didn't have to feel the pain that I saw in their eyes. To take away the terror I saw in the world, I tried: meditating, juice fasting, bananas, sugar, herbs, salt baths, smudging sage, swimming, surfing, dirt-bike riding, smoking pot, riding horses, calling in angels for protection, yoga, putting gold light around me, reading, Netflix binges, countless hours of Audible and podcast listening. All of them helped sustain me into normalcy. What has helped me the most? The woods, Audible, swimming, meditating, bananas, juicing, and spiritual protection are all a part of my daily routine, with some of the others mixed in.

To be a great psychic, one has to know themselves. Know your thoughts, feelings, and associations, so that you can decipher what's streaming through your consciousness. One has to be committed to self-growth and climb that ladder of self-discovery. One must be able say to himself, herself, or others, "I got it wrong. I am sorry. I messed up." Or, "It wasn't my fault. What can I learn from this in order to help myself and others out of suffering?"

I have never had a problem with having compassion for others' plights, but this, too, is a lesson. It's important to have boundaries on how others' actions affect you. Whether it's a person who is not dealing with their own stuff or a dog who is acting aggressively on a walk, there should still be boundaries. Once I realized that others' pasts are not an excuse to stay in the pattern of bad behavior, some people drifted away, while others started to show up in unexpected ways. People respected me, and the animals stepped into more peaceful roles. I was content, but I still wasn't living my fullest potential.

Because my heart was a sponge to suffering, I felt guilty for being happy when so many were hurting. I could rejoice in others' happiness, but felt guilty for my own. I realize now that we don't have to suffer with the world just because we are committed to helping it. Of course, there are times when the sadness overtakes us, but it doesn't have to rule us. Why didn't I see this before? I intellectually knew it, but I did not feel worthy of feeling my own joy.

I saw all the beauty in secret. The people who smile engaged in a passion, flowers that are blooming, the way the light shines off the ocean, the animals that are miraculously healing, the intense love I receive from people about my work, the way my spirit feels when I make love, meditate, surf, and swim, and how it feels to share an accomplishment or an awesome idea. Why did I hold that in secret, not letting it radiate from my heart?

I don't have to stay in the frequency of the suffering that I deal with daily. It's OK to experience more bliss than suffering. The pains of the world still matter if I go out into the world radiating joy.

Won't we be more productive working through hearts continually fueled by love rather than hearts constantly suffering with others? Do many of us need to ask ourselves this?

# "The Crane Wife" and "Before Point No Point"

Many months ago, I fell in love with a painting at the Primavera Art Gallery. It was thousands of dollars above my budget, but I snapped a photo of it anyway. The painting was of a small, box-shaped house that reminded me of a lighthouse. Ever since I was a young girl, I have always loved lighthouses. The idea that, even in stormy weather, a sailor could rely on a flashing light through the fog and the sound of a mariner's bell to alert them of home or rocky waters always calmed my restlessness. This house had its porch light on, another symbol to me of arriving home safely. Soon after I saw the painting, it started to show up in my visions during meditations. I would find myself walking up the steps into the house and then either upstairs or out the back door into mystical worlds or places to study.

One morning during my meditation, I found myself out the back door of the house. I had long, thin legs. Effortlessly, I took flight. I was a white crane flying over the waves at the edge of the water. I could smell and feel the spray of the ocean and sense the wind touching every muscle and feather, as I was lifted higher above the water. I flew through sunlight and puffy clouds in a world more vivid than this one, wishing it would never end. In a moment, I found myself landing in the arms of a man. I could feel his strong biceps supporting my bird body against his chest. He stroked my head and my back kindly. I pushed my head up against his cheek and wondered if this is how birds feel when they find themselves safe with a human friend. I looked down at my crane feet, and they morphed into webbed ones. Was I now a white duck or a goose? My conscience rose from the depth of my heart. I did not want to trick this man into believing I was solely a bird. I flew from his arms and turned around, using my will to turn me back into a woman. I felt the ocean fog around me and a white dress draped over my body. I wondered, *Do I now look like the ghost of a woman from an old movie?*

Then I was aware of my breath, the blanket around me, and my Chihuahua stirring to the rising sun out the bedroom window.

I went back to the gallery that day to visit the painting. It was thousands of dollars cheaper but still thousands more than I could spend. Months went by. Primavera closed. I wrote the artist telling her how much I loved her painting and made her an offer. The next day, she accepted. I was thrilled. We became friendly via email, both lovers of art and animals. A few days later, she wrote, "I made a big mistake! I thought the painting had been sent back ... Much to my surprise, it wasn't. I had two pieces of the lighthouses, and I thought the other one had been sold. I feel really bad! I am sending you another painting of a bird at no cost. This is called 'Crane Wife,' referring to one of my favorite folk tales of a Japanese wife who is a shape-shifter. The painting was hanging at the American Embassy in Kuwait for a couple of years, having been selected to be part of the Art in Embassy program."

I was stunned. The house was a lighthouse, after all. *Aw, it's gone. Did I read the email correctly? Is she gifting me a painting? Of a woman who shapeshifts into a crane? Words cannot express my sense of awe and gratitude.*

"The Crane Wife" is hanging by my front door. She stands just outside a door at the water's edge with the darkness behind her and light upon her chest. When I gaze at her, I am reminded of all that is safe and wonderful in this miraculous world.

★ "The Crane Wife" and the painting "Before Point No Point" are paintings by my new friend, Treacy Ziegler. You can find her work at: treacyziegler.com

# Chapter 8

# LAURA'S ANIMALS SPEAK

# An Easter Story for Any Time of Year

It is Easter Sunday 2017; the morning is still wet with mist. A hawk cries out in the distance. I scan the sky, but cannot find it. Hudson, my white German Shepherd, runs up ahead of me and into the woods. The hawk screeches again. *A warning?* I wonder and quickly locate Felix, my Chihuahua-mix and Luca, my Poodle. It is at this exact bend that I have seen a mountain lion leap into the air and climb only ten feet up an oak tree where he waited, asserting himself, by staring at me, swishing his tail slightly and digging his claws into the bark of the tree. Over the years, I have also seen foxes, coyotes, skunk, deer, owls, eagles, and bunnies cross the trail at this exact location.

The hawk is now flying over me. If I were taller, I could jump up and touch him. I admire the bands on his feathers and his red tail. He screeches again. My heart skips a beat. *Something is up. Should I be worried?*

I whistle for Hudson, who has disappeared for a little too long. He is trotting out of the woods now, and it looks as if Felix is running by his side. I look down, and Felix is at my heels.

Hudson has come out of the woods with another Chihuahua-mix in tow. She looks just like Felix, but skinnier, and her ears stick straight up instead of flopping over. I reach down to pet her. She stares up at me with marble-looking eyes. She's a bit mangy, so I am not generous with my affection.

I kneel down to talk with her. Hudson lies down to get close to her. Luca and Felix briefly sniff her and then lie down as well, telling her everything will be just fine.

"I don't know where my dad is," she says. "I think he threw me out of the car."

I take a deep breath and look her over. Her nails are all ripped and bloody, probably from hitting the pavement. "I'll take care of you. I promise," I say and lift her up to embrace her close to my heart. "Are you hungry or thirsty?"

"I ate poop and drank from a puddle," she told me, surprised by herself. "I slept with rabbits last night." Her eyes were weary, but stoic.

The little trouper finishes out our walk with us and jumps into the VW bus as if she were already part of the family. We go straight to Sunday brunch, where she eats turkey bacon and drinks from a glass. Later, she gets bathed and falls asleep wearing one of Felix's sweaters. The next day, we go to the vet. It's not mange. She's too skinny. Her nails all need to be pulled and bandaged — definitely from hitting the pavement. I locate her person by reading her chip. He doesn't want her anymore. Her name is Bella, but she doesn't answer to it. We call her "Easter Bunny." I tell her an angel told her person where to leave her so we would find her.

Easter's personality amazes me. She is happy all the time. She is scared only of thunder. There was thunder the night before we found her. But she is not scared of those woods. She actually loves to go there. She will chase the bunnies into the brush, and, while riding in the car, she will stick her head out the window like a bloodhound. Other dogs may be completely traumatized by being chucked out a moving car and left in the woods by their people, but Easter seems to go with the flow in a state of bliss.

"What is your secret?" I ask her.

She replies, "Trust that you are always loved. If you're lost, smell your way to someplace safe, and know that a friend will find you."

# Stay Calm and Carry On

My dogs give advice on how and why to remain calm when dealing with your pets.

Easter, my Chihuahua-mix, says, "You have to center yourself. If you don't, your animals will think you are crazy because your energy is scattered. Call your animal's name so they know you are speaking with them. Believe that your animal will hear you, otherwise, you are just talking at them. When you are calm inside of yourself, your animals want to be calm, too."

Luca, my Poodle, says, "You have to be calm yourself. If you yell at your animal, your animal will not trust you. You can stroke your animal when you want them to be calm. Don't be scared — ever. When people are scared, animals get freaked out. If you get scared, you should have a plan in your head, center yourself, visualize what you want, and do your plan without questioning it. Remember — nothing is a big deal. Life is fun." This is funny coming from Luca because he is kind of a serious, protective little guy. I am glad he is telling himself that "nothing is a big deal."

Felix says, "I know staying calm is hard to do sometimes. People can be spazzes. What I noticed is, you are what you think you are. If you start to freak out, something bad will happen. I notice this when I am in the car and you go into a store. If I get nervous that someone is going to talk to us through the window, it always happens. (I had to talk to him here about not worrying about being stolen and to enjoy people loving his cuteness.) The thing about worry is that sometimes you have lived a life where you have been forced to worry. Then you are living a great life, and, all of a sudden, you feel worry come up again. There is a part of you that is like "Stop thinking that," and then there is another part of you that is like, "I have to trust my intuition, and it's hard to know which is real."

I had to talk to him about this being life and to think of those moments as opportunities toward self-improvement. He thought about it for a moment and said, "You have to know life is awesome and that really nothing is that bad."

Hudson, my German Shepherd says, "The best way for people to be calm is to put their dogs in a down stay. Down stays are my fave, because they are like 'Whoa, energy. Relax.' People shouldn't expect too much from their pet, if they have not taught it to them. Everyone should know that your animals are way smarter than you think they are. You are a dumb-dumb if you don't train them. You have to train animals to know commands, otherwise they don't know how to listen to you. Everyone is like, 'Oh my animal is out of control.' But they don't want to deal with it.

"Talking with you makes me think. I love to think. If you love your animal, you'd better take the time to train them and talk with them. Otherwise, you may have a crazy animal."

# In Honor of Earth Day

In honor of Earth Day, I have asked my animals what they think of the Earth.

Luca, my seven-year-old Poodle, says, "After the fire, the Earth was really burnt and toxic to my paws and to my lungs, but now the land is getting green, and it smells fresh. Sometimes I feel sad for the Earth because I feel like people have too much garbage. My dog trainer and friend pick up garbage at the beach and parks. I find that to be nice for the world. I do notice that they are not just picking up poop, you know."

Easter, my four-year-old Chihuahua-mix, says, "I know the Earth's ocean. I feel you should do your part to protect it. I once saw a whale that was beached. It was really sad. It happened because humans didn't take care of the water environment. When I saw that suffering water animal, I got really sad in my heart. I think more people should know about this. People are amazing when they come together for a cause. I think they should help more whales."

Felix, my six-year-old Chihuahua-mix, says, "When I was young, I just knew pavement and a noisy world, but now

I know nature and quiet. I feel everyone should know nature and peace because it helps me get over trauma and know that I am safe. If you live in the city, take your dog to the park or for a road trip. My mom talks to animals all the time, and they are always asking for a green park. It will be a nice outing for you."

Clyde, my four-year-old Flemish Giant rabbit, says, "All rabbits should have outside time. I love morning-dew grass. I have lived in the high desert of Oregon, where the water is extremely pure, and I now live in a sacred valley, where there are mountains protecting us. I miss the clean water of Oregon. It tasted so good, but these mountains are beautiful, too. My advice to everyone is to be grateful for the Earth, where you live. If you notice it and enjoy it, you will be happier. I say this because I have known a lot of people who are so much in their head, they don't even see the beauty around them. That is silly, because it's beautiful where you are."

Ella, my five-year-old Snowshoe cat, says, "I love when the Earth smells fresh after a rain. I know that a lot of people take care of the Earth. This is important, because the healthier it is, the healthier we are who walk on it. Also, seeing is hard for me, because of the shadows, but when I am outside, I know the Earth beneath me. I feel everyone should walk the Earth with bare feet."

Seamora, my 26-year-old Blue and Gold Macaw, says, "I have a disability because I have a hurt wing and cannot fly. That is sad for me, because I am a bird that should fly most of the day. But my mom puts me outside daily. I walk and climb the yard for many hours. When you have a physical disability,

I think it's important to still move and enjoy your life. Even though where I live is not the tropics, I still enjoy the palm trees and the climbing roses. I don't like the cactuses. What I am trying to say is just because I can't fly the sky, it doesn't mean I can't enjoy the Earth. Make the most of what you have, and enjoy the smell of the roses."

Jubilee, my seven-year-old Warmblood/Appaloosa mare, says, "Being a horse, it's important for me to be able to run the Earth. My mom knows this. It's our nature to be able to run. Some horses are kept in little corrals. This is prison for them. I just want to say that, if you are going to have an animal, you should understand their true nature — what is in their soul and their cells. If you have to keep them in a little area, then make sure you find a way to let them be turned out to run the Earth. The Earth has a soul. When horses run, the soul of the Earth and the soul of the horse become one."

Hudson, my three-year-old white German Shepherd, says, "We all live on the Earth, so it's important to love it and take care of it. The Earth is what keeps us alive. I agree with Jubilee. When I run on the Earth, my soul and its soul become one. Unity is easier for animals than it is for people. People have to make a conscious effort to be meditative in nature. Make that time. Allow your life to flow more easily."

# What Family Means
## to My Animals

If you are reading this book, you probably feel pets are family. I wrote this article in honor of Mother's Day. I asked my animals what family means to them.

Felix, my seven-year-old Chihuahua-mix, says, "Family means a group of people and animals that you know, trust, and call your friend. If you try to bite them because you are scared, they forgive you."

Luca, my seven-year-old Poodle, says, "Family are people who teach you to be your best self. They know your potential, and they want you to live up to it."

Easter, my four-year-old Chihuahua-mix, says, "Family are people who don't want to get rid of you just because you have a behavior they don't like. They are always around to play and cuddle with. Family can even be friends of your people. It's someone who loves you no matter what."

Ella, my four-year-old Snowshoe cat, says, "A family member is someone who tries to figure you out when they realize something is wrong — like my person figured out that I see differently than others. I didn't even know that. Now I understand about shadows. Some family members you don't mind tolerating, and others are ones you want to know better."

Seamora, my 26-year-old Blue and Gold Macaw, says, "Family can include all different species. They don't have to be colorful — they just have to look you in the eyes and care."

Jubilee, my eight-year-old Appaloosa/Warmblood horse, says, "Family are groups that you feel comfortable with. They stand by you when you are scared or when you are learning something new. Family are others you feel safe with. If you have family you don't feel safe with, you should find friends that you do. They can be family, too."

Clyde, my four-year-old Flemish Giant rabbit, says, "Family are people and animals who laugh at your humor, enjoy the fun parts of you, and think you're are cute even when you are sleeping. If you have family that you feel only so-so with, imagine yourself with a family that adores you. I did that, and I got a new family. Don't worry about how it is going to happen; just know that you are worth being loved."

Hudson, my three-year-old white German Shepherd, says, "Family are beings that help you get your needs met. They sacrifice their own schedule so that you can learn, get better, or have fun exercise time. They are others that believe you can be better than you are. Families sometimes argue, but, after a good nap, no one cares. If you are feeling irritated with your family, you have to find something you love to do and forget about them for a while. They either will show you they love you or not. If they don't show you they love you, find others who do."

Hudson continues, "The great thing about being alive is that you can create anything you want. The main idea is to follow love, play, learn, and eat well. When you do that, you will notice you have family around. Family are not just relatives, but I think you got that. Sometimes if I am confused, I go to the beach and run in the water. Somehow that erases my confusion so I can start over. I have a lot of family I love. I am lucky that way."

# Creations for the New Year

I t's always fun to ask my animals what they want to manifest for themselves in the coming year.

Luca, my eight-year-old medium male Poodle, says, "I am going to be more agile with my jumps and weaves, and, also, I am going to be more magical in my brain."

Felix, my seven-year-old Chihuahua-mix, says, "I am going to let more people pet me and let go of my fear. I am going to remember to control my energy. I am going to learn a lot more tricks."

Easter, my four-year-old Chihuahua-mix, says, "I want to learn to fly in my dreams. Also, I am going to go to the beach more."

Hudson, my three-and-a-half-year-old white German Shepherd, says, "I want to go to the beach more, too. I am going to bring out my wise self and have more playmates. I am also going to manifest my paws always being healthy after I run through the bushes."

Ella, my five-year-old Snowshoe cat, says, "I don't see very well, and this morning I could see birds with my internal eye. I am going to do that more. I am going to trust my heart's intuition more than my reactions. Also, I am going to get a new catnip-scratching carboard bed."

Seamora, my 27-year-old Blue and Gold Macaw, says, "I am going to learn more words and dance to more music. I am going to become good friends with the yellow-and-black bird that comes to eat my food and swim in the fountain outside. I am going to stand on my mom's shoulder more."

Clyde, my four-year-old Flemish Giant rabbit, says, "I am definitely going to learn how to race Hudson across the yard and win. I am going to make Felix be my friend. He is still standoffish, and my mom is going to get me a carboard house for inside."

Jubilee, my eight-year-old Appaloosa/Warmblood, says, "I am going to manifest my mom coming to Oregon to visit me more. I have everything I want, but I am going to be braver getting into the smaller trailers, and I am going to go on more trips to the mountains — and I have already mastered running in snow. My friend Phoenix (Mustang) and I are going to learn to jump over logs at the same time. We have been practicing. Oh, and I am going to be a good friend to a bunch of new Mustangs that don't know about people yet. When you know something, it's important to teach it to others. I learn a lot."

I have two Wooley Fire evacuees staying at my house until their home is cleaned from smoke damage. So, I have to include them, too.

Taffy, a 12-year-old Poodle-Terrier mix, says, "I have already started to believe that I can do more things than I thought I could. I can walk farther and play longer. Also, I want to spend more time visiting different nature places, and I also want to meet more species of animals. I want to go to the botanical gardens."

Dalhma, a 12-year-old cat, says, "I am blind, but I have started to use my internal eye to see things, and it's incredible. I feel energy and see colors that I didn't know existed. I am going to stretch more and also make sure I eat all the healthy food given to me. I am open to new possibilities, and I believe that people and animals have open hearts and want to help each other. I am going to send love out into the world and be thankful for the love that comes back to me."

# Words of Wisdom from My Late Australian Shepherd, Stormy

My late Australian Shepherd, Stormy, was born June 14, 1999, and died March 5, 2015. He was black and white. I picked him out when he was two days old so that he could keep his tail. He was the first to bark and the first to venture away from his litter of ten. Even as a young puppy, he was able to tame Maia, my aggressive Wolf-hybrid, into loving him. Stormy was perfect from the start. Not only did he learn all his commands fast, but he had a nature that radiated love and kindness to all he met. Kids at the park thought he was a teddy bear/dog hybrid because of the way he would ramble up to them. He marched himself into hospitals, charming the sick and depressed into smiles. His soft-spoken, bright eyes and wagging tail gained him access into every convention center I ever spoke at. His column in the local paper and his words of wisdom at the end of The Pet Psychic Radio Show built him a huge fan club. He received emails, snail mail, presents, and shouts of love out of car windows.

I thought that today, I would share some of his words of wisdom:

*"If you feel yourself being negative, you have to remember that love is big. Love is bigger than all of us. If you can find a little bit inside of you and concentrate on that, eventually you'll feel the enormity of it."*

— STORMY (23/MAY/2013)

*"The most important thing when anyone is sick is to imagine their blueprint of health. It's so important. Imagine what it feels like and looks like to be healthy. If you do that, eventually you will be healthy."*

— STORMY (10/JAN/2013)

*"If you have a disability or a mental problem, put your chin up, take one step at a time, and enjoy yourself. The more you do that, you'll see you'll make a friend. It's easier to walk with a friend."*

— STORMY (6/JUN/2013)

*"It is important to see yourself as a Light. The brighter you express your Light, the more beings are affected by your Radiance. If you feel dark, shelter yourself. It takes only a few moments to rest and allow the Light to radiate again. Everyone has Light in them. Some people ignore it. Be the Light."*

— STORMY (22/AUG/2013)

*"Take a moment and think to yourself about what feels good inside of you. Healing energy comes from your heart center. Think about, in your heart, how your life is and what makes your heart grow.*

*Then be disciplined. If you have a hard time being disciplined, have a calendar that you see every day, and then make sure every day you do something to make your heart bigger."*

— STORMY (26/DEC/2013)

*"Listen to your animal with Joy. When you're thinking about them, think about them in Joy. Because Joy is the center of the heart."*

— STORMY (24/APR/2014)

*"I have to tell everybody that it's important to spend time with yourself. I know that it's all about the animals. But if you don't take care of you, your animals will suffer. If you're stressed around them, they might get sick."*

— STORMY (1/MAY/2014)

*"Stop not believing in your animal's health. Believe that they can get better. Miracles happen every day, and God or the Universe grants miracles to everyone."*

— STORMY (17/JUL/2014)

*"One of the things that you can all do is sit with your animal and send Love to them. If you do that every day, you'll be able to hear them better. Just at the end of when you're sending the Love, that's when their voice will pop into your head."*

— STORMY (30/MAY/2013)

To read more of Stormy's quotes read
my book, *Stormy's Words of Wisdom:*
An enlightened dog's profound insights on life.

# Not Just Catnip and Dog Biscuits: Animals Share Their Definitions of Love

I ask my animals, "What is love?"

Ella, my cat, says, "Love is finding your purpose after you have been hurt. Love is comfortable bedding and playing every day. Love is the space within you and around you that creates amazing things in your life. Love is my life. I am love."

Felix, my Chihuahua-mix, says, "Love is a mystery that flows through all things. It is what brings rescue animals to their people and wild animals to safety during a fire. It is a spirit rising within you."

Easter, my other Chihuahua-mix, says, "Love is cuddles and songs that people sing to you. Love is a good meal and being happy for no reason. Love is when you smell good and people like to kiss you."

Seamora, my Blue and Gold Macaw, says, "Love is when I share my food with the wild birds and let them bathe in the fountain before me. Love is definitely music and the sound of the wind through the trees. Love is awesome. If you think you don't have it, you are wrong. It's everywhere — you just have to notice it."

Clyde, my Flemish Giant rabbit, says, "Love is the energy that helps you manifest what you want. Love is being grateful. It is carrot tops and lots of friends. It's when my mom laughs at me for being naughty instead of scolding me. It's also when she takes the time to explain why she needs me to be good. Love is clear communication and patience. It is also enjoying a ripe banana."

Jubilee, my Appaloosa/Warmblood horse, says, "Love is having a best friend you can trust in all situations. If you get it wrong, they may get it right. Love is knowing yourself and being brave enough to trust others even if someone has hurt you in the past. Love is jumping over tree limbs in the snow. Love is someone taking the time to scratch your butt with a rake even though their own back is sore."

Hudson, my white German Shepherd, says, "Love is traveling through the Universe to find someone you love deeply. Love is being grateful for what is around you. Love is much more than you think it is. It's what all things wonderful are created from. I also want to say that love is chasing deer and squirrels, but my mom won't like that one. Mom said it may be the speed and sense of direct focus I like. Ohh ... Love is morning snuggles in bed. Those are the best."

Luca, my Poodle, says, "Love is a wonderful feeling that allows you to be happy when there are difficult things happening. It's sunshine all the time. It is also what you have for yourself."

**LAURA STINCHFIELD**

# ThePetPsychic.com
### Teaching The Conscious Bond™

## If you enjoyed this book, please support me by writing a review.

Like all authors, I rely on online reviews to encourage future sales.

Your opinion is invaluable. Would you take a few moments now to share your assessment of my book on Amazon or any other book-review website you prefer?

Your opinion will help the book marketplace become more transparent and useful to all.

It will also help spread the consciousness of animals. The more aware people are of the thoughts and feelings of animals, the better they will be treated.

Thank you!

Take care and be well!

You can also find me at:
*www.ThePetPsychic.com*
*www.facebook.com/PetPsychicRadio*
*www.youtube.com/petpsychic*
*Instagram @thepetpsychic*

## ALSO BY LAURA STINCHFIELD

Stormy's Words of Wisdom
*An enlightened dog's profound insights on life.*

CPSIA information can be obtained
at www.ICGtesting.com
Printed in the USA
LVHW050758130920
665829LV00016B/2104